The Artificial Intelligence Takeover

How AI is Redefining Humanity's Future

Avery T. Smith

I0441154

Table of Contents

Introduction: The Dawn of the AI Era

Brief History of AI

The story of artificial intelligence is not a recent one, but rather a tale that spans decades, interwoven with the dreams and aspirations of visionaries, scientists, and thinkers. The concept of creating machines that could mimic human intelligence has been a part of human imagination for centuries. Ancient myths from various cultures spoke of statues that could come to life or mechanical beings with human-like qualities. However, the scientific journey of AI began in earnest in the mid-20th century.

In the 1950s, the term "artificial intelligence" was coined by John McCarthy, a young computer scientist who, along with his colleagues, embarked on the ambitious quest to create machines that could think. The Dartmouth Conference of 1956 is often hailed as the birthplace of AI as a field of study. Here, pioneers like McCarthy, Marvin Minsky, and Alan Newell laid the foundational ideas that would drive AI research for decades to come.

The subsequent years saw a roller-coaster of progress and setbacks. The 1960s and 70s witnessed the first wave of AI optimism, with significant funding and research leading to early successes in areas like natural language processing and problem-solving algorithms. However, by the 1980s, the initial enthusiasm met with reality checks, leading to the first "AI winter," a period of reduced funding and skepticism about the field's promises.

Despite these challenges, the flame of AI innovation never truly extinguished. The 1990s and early 2000s saw the emergence of machine learning, neural networks, and the seeds of today's deep learning revolution. With the advent of big data, increased computational power, and refined algorithms, the 2010s marked a renaissance for AI. Technologies that were once mere concepts—self-driving cars, virtual assistants, and game-playing AIs—began to materialize, transforming the landscape of technology and society.

As we reflect on this rich tapestry of AI's history, it becomes evident that the journey was never just about machines. It was, and continues to be, a reflection of humanity's insatiable curiosity and our relentless drive to push the boundaries of the possible.

The past has set the stage, but the significance of AI in today's world is unparalleled. As we stand on the precipice of a new era, it's essential to understand how deeply AI has permeated our lives and what it signifies for our collective future.

In the modern era, the influence of artificial intelligence is omnipresent, shaping industries, redefining interactions, and transforming the very fabric of society. Its significance is not just in the groundbreaking technological advancements it brings, but in the profound impact it has on human lives, economies, cultures, and global dynamics.

Economic Transformation: At the heart of the global economy, AI-driven automation and data analytics are revolutionizing industries. From manufacturing to finance, AI algorithms optimize processes, predict market trends, and personalize consumer experiences. The result is increased efficiency, innovative products, and new business models. However, with this comes the challenge of job displacement and the need for workforce reskilling, underscoring the dual-edged nature of AI's economic influence.

Healthcare Revolution: In the realm of healthcare, AI is a beacon of hope and innovation. Machine learning models assist in diagnosing diseases with precision, sometimes outperforming human experts. AI-driven drug discovery accelerates the development of life-saving medications, and personalized medicine tailors treatments to individual genetic profiles, heralding a new age of medical care.

Social Dynamics: On the social front, AI shapes our daily interactions. Virtual assistants like Siri or Alexa have become household names, and recommendation algorithms on platforms like Netflix or Spotify curate personalized entertainment experiences. Yet, there's a trade-off: concerns about privacy, data security, and the potential for AI to perpetuate societal biases.

Cultural Impact: Culturally, AI challenges our perceptions of creativity and art. Algorithms now compose music, create artwork, and even write poetry, prompting us to reflect on the essence of human creativity and its distinction from machine-generated content.

Global Implications: On a global scale, AI is a powerful tool in addressing pressing challenges, from climate change modeling to humanitarian aid distribution. However, it also presents geopolitical challenges, with nations vying for AI supremacy, leading to potential power imbalances and ethical dilemmas.

As we navigate this AI-augmented world, it's evident that its significance is multifaceted, bringing forth opportunities and challenges in equal measure. It's not just a technological marvel but a mirror reflecting humanity's aspirations, dilemmas, and the eternal quest for progress.

"The Artificial Intelligence Takeover: How AI is Redefining Humanity's Future" delves deep into the world of AI, unraveling its history, its present influence, and its potential future impacts. This book is not just a chronicle of technological advancements but a comprehensive exploration of AI's profound influence on various facets of human existence.

You will embark on a journey that traverses the economic transformations brought about by AI, its revolutionary impact on healthcare, its role in reshaping social dynamics, and its cultural implications. The book also addresses the ethical challenges posed by AI, from concerns about privacy and data security to the broader societal implications of unchecked AI development.

Through detailed chapters, expert insights, and real-world case studies, this book offers a holistic view of the AI landscape. It serves as both a guide for those unfamiliar with the field and a reflection for experts, policymakers, and thinkers. By the end, you will gain a nuanced understanding of AI's role in shaping the present and sculpting the future, equipped with the knowledge to navigate the AI-augmented world with awareness and responsibility.

Chapter 1: Foundations of Artificial Intelligence

Definition and Types of AI

Artificial Intelligence, often abbreviated as AI, is a term that has been both a source of wonder and confusion for many. At its core, AI refers to the simulation of human intelligence processes by machines, especially computer systems. These processes include learning, reasoning, self-correction, and problem-solving. But to truly grasp the essence of AI, it's crucial to delve deeper into its various types and classifications.

1. **Narrow or Weak AI:** This is the most common form of AI that we encounter in our daily lives. Narrow AI is designed and trained for a specific task. Virtual personal assistants, like Apple's Siri or Amazon's Alexa, are prime examples. They operate under a predefined set or rules and don't possess consciousness or emotions. They are incredibly adept at the tasks they're designed for but are limited in their scope.

2. **General or Strong AI:** This form of AI is still largely theoretical and represents a machine that has the ability to perform any intellectual task that a human being can. It's a more extensive and holistic form of AI, possessing human-like abilities to understand, learn, and apply knowledge, reason through problems, have

consciousness, and even potentially possess emotional understanding.

3. **Artificial Superintelligence (ASI):** This is the advancement of General AI. ASI refers to a situation where machines surpass human abilities across the board. It represents machines that aren't just mimicking or replicating human intelligence and behaviors but surpassing them. The discussions around ASI often tread into philosophical territories, raising questions about humanity, consciousness, and the very nature of existence.

Beyond these broad classifications, AI can be categorized based on functionalities:

- **Reactive Machines:** These are basic AI systems that don't have past memories and can't use past experiences to inform future decisions. IBM's chess-playing Deep Blue, which beat international grandmaster Garry Kasparov, is an example.

- **Limited Memory:** These AI systems can use past experiences to inform future actions. Most contemporary AI, including the AI that runs self-driving cars, falls into this category.

- **Theory of Mind:** This classification is still theoretical and represents machines that understand emotions, beliefs, and other human mental processes.

- **Self-aware AI:** This is an advanced form of AI that has its consciousness, similar to human awareness. It's still a concept and hasn't been realized yet.

As we navigate the vast landscape of AI definitions and types, it becomes evident that AI isn't just a monolithic entity but a spectrum of technologies, each with its capabilities, limitations, and potential. The journey of AI from theoretical constructs to tangible technologies has been marked by the relentless pursuit of knowledge, innovation, and a vision for a better future. This journey, however, wouldn't have been possible without the trailblazers who dared to dream and transform those dreams into reality.

The foundations of AI, as we understand and experience it today, were laid by visionaries who, decades ago, foresaw a world where machines could mimic, and even surpass, human intelligence. Their groundbreaking work, seminal experiments, and indomitable spirit charted the course for the AI revolution.

Early Pioneers and Milestones

The history of artificial intelligence is a tapestry of brilliant minds, groundbreaking ideas, and pivotal moments that have collectively shaped the trajectory of the field. While AI as a concept has ancient roots in mythology and philosophy, its scientific journey began in the 20th century.

Alan Turing and the Turing Test (1940s):

Arguably the father of theoretical computer science and artificial intelligence, Alan Turing introduced the concept of the "Universal Machine" that could compute anything computable. His 1950 paper, "Computing Machinery and Intelligence," posed the provocative question, "Can machines think?" This led to the formulation of the Turing Test, a measure of a machine's ability to exhibit intelligent behavior indistinguishable from that of a human. Though the Turing Test has its critics, it set the stage for decades of AI research.

John von Neumann (1940s-1950s):

Von Neumann made significant contributions to the development of the digital computer and cellular automata. His architecture, the "von Neumann architecture," became the foundational layout for most subsequent computer designs.

The Birth of AI - The Dartmouth Workshop (1956):

Organized by John McCarthy, Marvin Minsky, Nathaniel Rochester, and Claude Shannon, this workshop is often considered the birthplace of AI as a field of study. It was here that the term "artificial intelligence" was coined and adopted.

Frank Rosenblatt and the Perceptron (1957):

Rosenblatt introduced the Perceptron, the first neural network for computers, which simulated the thought processes of the human brain. Though its capabilities were limited, it laid the groundwork for future research in neural networks.

Marvin Minsky and John McCarthy (1960s):

Both made significant contributions during the early days of AI. Minsky's work on neural nets led to the development of the first head-mounted graphical display, while McCarthy developed the Lisp programming language, which became the standard AI programming language.

ELIZA - The First Chatbot (1964-1966):

Developed by Joseph Weizenbaum at MIT, ELIZA was an early natural language processing computer program. Its most famous mode, DOCTOR, simulated a Rogerian psychotherapist and used scripts to mimic human conversation.

Shakey the Robot (1966-1972):

Developed at Stanford Research Institute, Shakey was the first general-purpose mobile robot able to reason about its actions. It combined research in robotics, computer vision, and natural language processing, marking a significant advancement in AI integration.

The "AI Winter" (1970s-1980s):

Despite the early enthusiasm, AI research faced significant challenges, leading to reduced funding and skepticism about its promises. This period, termed the "AI Winter," was marked by a re-evaluation of the field's goals and methodologies.

Expert Systems and MYCIN (1970s):

The development of expert systems, computer programs that mimic the decision-making abilities of a human expert, marked a resurgence in AI interest. MYCIN, one of the earliest expert systems, was designed to diagnose bacterial infections and recommend antibiotics.

Backpropagation (1980s):

Introduced by Geoffrey Hinton, backpropagation became a fundamental concept in training artificial neural networks. This technique adjusted the weights of neurons to minimize the difference between the predicted and actual output.

Deep Blue Defeats Kasparov (1997):

In a landmark moment for AI, IBM's Deep Blue defeated world chess champion Garry Kasparov. This event showcased the potential of AI in problem-solving tasks previously thought to be the domain of human experts.

The pioneers of AI were not just technologists but visionaries who foresaw a world where machines could augment human capabilities. Their contributions, both theoretical and practical, laid the groundwork for the AI-driven world we live in today. As we delve deeper into the nuances of AI in subsequent chapters, it's essential to remember and honor the foundational work of these trailblazers.

Chapter 2: Technological Breakthroughs and Milestones

Major Advancements in AI Research

The evolution of artificial intelligence is a testament to human ingenuity and relentless pursuit of knowledge. From its conceptual origins to its modern-day manifestations, AI research has witnessed a series of groundbreaking advancements that have redefined the boundaries of what machines can achieve. Here's a detailed exploration of these pivotal moments in AI research:

Neural Networks and the Concept of Machine Learning (1940s-1960s):

The idea of creating machines that could mimic the neural structures of the human brain led to the development of artificial neural networks. Early models, like the perceptron introduced by Frank Rosenblatt in 1957, were rudimentary but set the stage for more complex multi-layered networks. These networks laid the foundation for machine learning, where machines could learn from data without being explicitly programmed.

Evolution of Algorithms (1970s-1980s):

The growth of AI was intrinsically linked to the sophistication of algorithms. Algorithms like the ID3 (Iterative Dichotomiser 3) for decision tree learning and the development of the k-nearest neighbors algorithm for pattern recognition played crucial roles in enhancing machine learning capabilities.

The Rise of Probabilistic Models (1980s-1990s):

The realization that uncertainty and probabilistic reasoning could enhance AI's decision-making capabilities led to the development of Bayesian networks and Hidden Markov Models. These models allowed machines to make predictions and decisions even when faced with incomplete or uncertain data.

Support Vector Machines (1990s):

Introduced in the 1990s, Support Vector Machines (SVM) became a popular machine learning model for classification and regression tasks. Its ability to handle high-dimensional data and its versatility made it a mainstay in AI research.

Reinforcement Learning and Decision Making (1990s-2000s):

Reinforcement learning, where machines learn by interacting with their environment and receiving feedback, gained prominence. Algorithms like Q-learning allowed machines to optimize decision-making over time, paving the way for applications like game-playing AIs and robotics.

Deep Learning Revolution (2010s-Present):

Building on the foundations of neural networks, deep learning introduced multi-layered neural networks known as deep neural networks. Pioneers like Geoffrey Hinton, Yann LeCun, and Yoshua Bengio advanced this subfield, leading to breakthroughs in image and speech recognition. The introduction of architectures like Convolutional Neural Networks (CNNs) and Recurrent Neural Networks (RNNs) further propelled deep learning to the forefront of AI research.

Transfer Learning and Pre-trained Models (2010s-Present):

The idea that AI models could transfer knowledge from one task to another led to the development of transfer learning techniques. Pre-trained models, which are trained on vast datasets and then fine-tuned for specific tasks, became instrumental in democratizing AI, allowing researchers with limited resources to achieve state-of-the-art results.

Generative Adversarial Networks (GANs) (2010s-Present):

Introduced by Ian Goodfellow and his colleagues in 2014, GANs consist of two neural networks – a generator and a discriminator – that work in tandem to produce highly realistic data. GANs have found applications in image generation, style transfer, and more.

Transformers and Natural Language Processing (2010s-Present):

The transformer architecture, introduced in the paper "Attention is All You Need" by Vaswani et al. in 2017, revolutionized natural language processing. Models like BERT, GPT, and T5, built on transformer architectures, set new benchmarks in tasks like language translation, question-answering, and text generation.

Quantum Computing and AI (2010s-Present):

The intersection of quantum computing and AI is a burgeoning field. Quantum algorithms have the potential to solve complex problems exponentially faster than classical algorithms, offering promising avenues for AI's future.

Edge Computing and AI (2010s-Present):

With the proliferation of IoT devices and the need for real-time processing, AI began moving closer to the data source. Edge computing allows AI models to run directly on local devices, from smartphones to industrial machines, reducing latency and ensuring faster decision-making. This shift not only enhances efficiency but also addresses concerns related to data privacy and bandwidth costs.

Federated Learning (2010s-Present):

A novel approach to machine learning, federated learning enables model training across multiple devices or servers while keeping the data localized. It's a significant step towards privacy-preserving AI, as raw data doesn't need to be centralized, reducing the risk of data breaches.

Explainable AI (XAI) (2010s-Present):

As AI systems become more intricate, understanding their decision-making processes becomes crucial, especially in sectors like healthcare or finance where stakes are high. XAI aims to make AI's decisions transparent, interpretable, and understandable to humans, bridging the gap between machine operations and human intuition.

Neurosymbolic AI (2010s-Present):

While neural networks excel at pattern recognition, symbolic AI is adept at reasoning. Neurosymbolic AI combines the strengths of both, aiming to create systems that can learn from data and reason over it. This hybrid approach holds promise for more robust and versatile AI systems.

AI Ethics and Fairness (2010s-Present):

With AI's growing influence, concerns about its ethical implications have come to the forefront. Research in this domain focuses on ensuring AI systems are fair, transparent, and devoid of biases. Tools and frameworks are being developed to audit AI models, ensuring they align with ethical standards and societal values.

AI for Social Good (2010s-Present):

Beyond commercial applications, AI has shown immense potential in addressing global challenges. From predicting natural disasters to aiding in wildlife conservation, from enhancing accessibility for the differently-abled to providing educational tools for underprivileged regions, AI's role in societal betterment is ever-expanding.

Synthetic Media and Deepfakes (2010s-Present):

AI's capability to generate hyper-realistic media, be it images, videos, or audio, has given rise to both awe-inspiring applications and concerns. While synthetic media can aid in content creation, deepfakes pose challenges related to misinformation and security.

AI in Cybersecurity (2010s-Present):

As cyber threats evolve, AI has become an indispensable tool in cybersecurity. From detecting anomalies to predicting potential threats, AI-enhanced security systems offer robust protection in an increasingly digital world.

Human-AI Collaboration (2010s-Present):

The future of AI isn't about machines replacing humans but working alongside them. Research in human-AI collaboration focuses on creating systems that augment human capabilities, ensuring a symbiotic relationship where both entities learn from and complement each other.

AI Hardware and Custom Chips (2010s-Present):

With increasing computational demands, there's a shift towards designing hardware optimized for AI operations. Companies are developing custom chips, like TPUs (Tensor Processing Units), to accelerate AI tasks, ensuring faster and more efficient processing.

AI in Healthcare (2010s-Present):

The medical field has been one of the most significant beneficiaries of AI advancements. From diagnostic AI that can detect diseases in medical imagery with precision rivaling or even surpassing human experts, to predictive analytics that can forecast patient needs or potential outbreaks, AI is revolutionizing healthcare. Drug discovery, too, has been expedited with AI models predicting molecular interactions.

Natural Language Processing (NLP) and Translation (2000s-Present):

The dream of machines understanding and generating human language took a significant leap with advanced NLP techniques. Tools like Google Translate, which can instantly translate between numerous languages, have bridged communication gaps globally. Sentiment analysis, chatbots, and personal assistants like Siri and Alexa also owe their existence to NLP advancements.

AI in Autonomous Vehicles (2010s-Present):

The automotive industry is undergoing a transformation with the integration of AI. From Tesla's Autopilot to Waymo's self-driving cars, AI algorithms process vast amounts of data in real-time to make split-second decisions, bringing the dream of autonomous vehicles closer to reality.

AI in Finance (2010s-Present):

The financial sector leverages AI for fraud detection, robo-advisors, algorithmic trading, and personalized banking experiences. AI's predictive analytics capabilities enable the forecasting of stock market trends, credit scoring, and automation of mundane tasks, revolutionizing the financial landscape.

Swarm Intelligence and Robotics (2010s-Present):

Drawing inspiration from nature, where birds flock and fish school, swarm intelligence in AI focuses on the collective behavior of decentralized systems. This has led to advancements in robotics where multiple robots collaborate to perform tasks, showcasing potential applications in agriculture, logistics, and even space exploration.

Augmented Reality (AR) and Virtual Reality (VR) with AI (2010s-Present):

AR and VR technologies, when combined with AI, offer immersive experiences that are intelligent and interactive. From gaming to professional training simulations, AI-driven AR and VR applications are creating hyper-realistic virtual worlds that respond to user inputs in real-time.

AI in Agriculture and Climate Change (2010s-Present):

AI-driven solutions in agriculture, such as precision farming, help in optimizing yields and resource usage. Furthermore, AI models are being used to predict climate patterns, helping in the formulation of strategies to combat climate change.

AI-driven Content Creation (2010s-Present):

From AI-generated art and music to tools that assist in content writing and video production, AI is making waves in the creative industry. Platforms like DeepArt and Jukebox by OpenAI showcase the potential of AI in artistic endeavors.

AI in Space Exploration (2010s-Present):

Space agencies are leveraging AI for various tasks, from analyzing vast amounts of astronomical data to autonomous navigation of spacecraft. AI-driven robots and rovers are being envisioned for future interplanetary missions.

AI's Role in Pandemic Response (2020s):

The global response to the COVID-19 pandemic saw AI playing a crucial role, from tracking the spread of the virus to aiding in vaccine research. Predictive models helped policymakers make informed decisions, showcasing AI's potential in global health crises.

The tapestry of AI research and its advancements is vast and ever-evolving. Each innovation not only pushes the boundaries of technological capabilities but also reshapes our societal structures, economies, and daily lives. As we stand on the cusp of further breakthroughs, it's essential to reflect on the practical implications of these advancements.

While the milestones in AI research provide a theoretical backdrop, the real testament to AI's transformative power lies in its practical applications. The next section will delve deep into real-world case studies, shedding light on how AI has been a game-changer across various domains.

Case Studies of Groundbreaking AI Applications

Healthcare: The Eye-Opening Tale of Diabetic Retinopathy Detection

You know, there's a silent threat out there, lurking in the shadows, called diabetic retinopathy. It's this eye condition that can sneak up on folks with diabetes, and if left unchecked, it can lead to blindness. Now, here's where it gets interesting. In many parts of the world, especially remote areas, getting an eye check-up by a specialist isn't a walk in the park. But guess who's coming to the rescue? Good ol' AI. Google, being the tech giant it is, decided to tackle this head-on. They trained a deep learning system using thousands of retinal images. The result? An AI that could spot the early signs of this condition as accurately as seasoned eye doctors. Think about the implications! This isn't just tech for tech's sake; it's about giving people a fighting chance to protect their sight.

Conservation: The Wildbook Chronicles

Alright, picture this: vast landscapes, teeming with wildlife. Zebras grazing, cheetahs prowling, and amidst all this, conservationists with a Herculean task— tracking and monitoring these creatures. Manual tracking? It's like finding a zebra-striped needle in a haystack. Enter "Wildbook." It's this innovative project that's like a social network, but for animals. Snap a photo of a zebra or a whale, upload it, and the AI does its magic. It identifies the individual animal, logs it, and even tracks its movements over time. This isn't just cool tech; it's a lifeline for endangered species. By understanding animal populations and migrations, we can make informed conservation decisions. It's tech meeting ecology in the best possible way.

Agriculture: Drones to the Rescue!

Farming's tough. It's not just about sowing seeds and hoping for the best. There are pests, diseases, and a myriad of challenges that farmers face daily. Now, imagine having a bird's-eye view of everything, with an added layer of AI intelligence. Companies like Aerobotics are doing just that. They've got these drones that fly over fields, capturing detailed images. But here's the kicker: the AI analyzes these images in real-time. It can spot a section of crops that's under stress, detect early signs of pest infestations, and even predict yield. For farmers, this is a game-changer. It's about being proactive, addressing issues before they balloon into bigger problems. And at the heart of it all? AI, working tirelessly, ensuring our food sources are secure and thriving.

Art & Creativity: The Enigma of "Edmond de Belamy"

Art, for the longest time, has been the realm of human expression, right? But then came along "Edmond de Belamy," a portrait with a twist. This wasn't the work of a master artist holed up in a studio. No, this was the brainchild of a Generative Adversarial Network (GAN). The art world was abuzz! Here was a portrait, every brushstroke generated by an AI, and it was so compelling that it fetched a whopping $432,000 at Christie's. Beyond the price tag, it sparked a profound debate. What is creativity? Can machines possess it? While purists argue that art is a deeply human endeavor, there's no denying that AI has opened up a Pandora's box, challenging our very notions of creativity and artistic value.

Disaster Response: AI, the Earthquake Whisperer

Mother Nature is unpredictable, and earthquakes are her most elusive mysteries. For years, scientists have grappled with predicting aftershocks, those tremors that follow the main quake. Enter AI. A collaboration between Harvard and Google saw deep learning algorithms being trained on a vast database of seismic activity. The result? An AI that could predict aftershock locations with uncanny accuracy. While it's not a crystal ball predicting exact times and magnitudes, it's a significant leap. Such predictions can guide evacuation plans, building designs, and emergency responses, potentially saving countless lives.

Finance: AI's Detective Stint in Banking

The world of finance, with its vast transactions and intricate networks, has always been a prime target for fraudsters. But banks have a new ally in their corner: AI. Picture this: every time you swipe your card or make an online transaction, there's an AI system, like Kount, vigilantly scanning the details. It's looking for patterns, anomalies, anything that smells fishy. And it learns, oh how it learns! With every transaction, it gets smarter, understanding your spending habits, and raising a red flag if something's amiss. It's not just about safeguarding money; it's about trust. In a digital age, where faceless transactions are the norm, AI ensures that trust isn't compromised.

These tales of AI's foray into various domains showcase its transformative power. But as we marvel at these innovations, it's essential to understand the broader implications. How is AI shaping economies, influencing job markets, and redefining industries?

As we pull back from individual stories, we're faced with a larger narrative. AI isn't just a tool; it's an economic force, reshaping industries, creating new ones, and redefining the very nature of work. But what does this mean for economies, for workers, and for the future of work? Dive into Chapter 3 as we explore the economic tapestry being woven by AI.

Chapter 3: Economic Impacts of AI

The integration of artificial intelligence into the global economic fabric is both profound and pervasive. As we traverse this chapter, we will meticulously dissect the multifaceted influence of AI across a spectrum of industries, from manufacturing to entertainment, and its subsequent ramifications on the job market. The confluence of AI with traditional economic structures is not just reshaping paradigms but also redefining the future of work and production.

AI's Transformative Role Across Industries

Manufacturing:

The manufacturing sector stands as a testament to AI's transformative power. Modern factories are increasingly shifting from manual labor to AI-driven automation. For instance, Tesla's Gigafactory, with its advanced robotics, epitomizes this evolution, where robots handle tasks ranging from assembly to quality control, ensuring precision and efficiency.

Agriculture:

Agriculture, one of humanity's oldest professions, is being revitalized by AI. Precision farming techniques, underpinned by AI, ensure optimal utilization of resources. For instance, John Deere's AI-equipped tractors can detect and spray only weed-infested areas, reducing chemical usage and ensuring healthier crops.

Supply Chain and Logistics:

DHL, a global logistics leader, employs AI to predict shipment delays, optimizing routes and ensuring timely deliveries. Similarly, AI-driven demand forecasting tools are becoming indispensable for retailers, ensuring they maintain optimal stock levels, reducing wastage, and enhancing profitability.

Healthcare:

Beyond diagnostics, AI is revolutionizing patient care. IBM's Watson can analyze the meaning and context of structured and unstructured data in clinical notes and reports. Such systems aid doctors in diagnosing diseases, suggesting treatments, and even predicting patient needs.

Energy:

In the energy sector, AI-driven predictive maintenance tools are ensuring infrastructural efficiency. Companies like GE employ AI to predict equipment failures in power plants, leading to increased operational efficiency and reduced downtimes.

Retail:

Amazon, a retail behemoth, employs AI for demand forecasting, product recommendation, and customer service. Their cashier-less "Go" stores use AI to track and bill products, eliminating the need for traditional checkouts.

Finance:

Goldman Sachs uses AI to analyze vast datasets for investment opportunities, while AI-driven chatbots, like Bank of America's Erica, assist customers with queries, ensuring efficient and personalized service.

Entertainment:

Netflix's recommendation engine, powered by AI, analyzes user behavior to suggest shows and movies, ensuring increased viewer engagement. Similarly, Spotify's Discover Weekly playlist employs AI to curate songs tailored to individual user tastes.

Real Estate:

AI-driven platforms like Zillow employ algorithms to provide property value estimates, aiding buyers and sellers in making informed decisions. Similarly, AI tools are being used to predict real estate market trends, guiding investors.

Tourism and Hospitality:

Hotel chains like Marriott are employing AI-driven chatbots for room bookings, while platforms like Kayak use AI to predict flight prices, aiding travelers in making cost-effective decisions.

Education:

The education sector is witnessing a paradigm shift with the integration of AI. Platforms like Coursera and Khan Academy use AI to track student progress, offering personalized learning paths based on individual strengths and weaknesses. Furthermore, AI-driven chatbots assist students with queries, providing 24/7 support. In classrooms, AI tools like Squirrel AI offer personalized tutoring, adapting content in real-time based on student responses.

Transportation:

The transportation industry is on the cusp of a revolution with the advent of autonomous vehicles. Companies like Waymo and Tesla are at the forefront, developing self-driving cars that employ AI to process vast amounts of data in real-time, making split-second decisions that can prevent accidents. In urban planning, AI algorithms analyze traffic patterns to optimize traffic light timings, reducing congestion.

Construction and Urban Planning:

AI is playing a pivotal role in modern construction methodologies. Tools like ALICE employ AI to optimize construction schedules, ensuring timely project completion and cost efficiency. In urban planning, AI-driven simulations predict the impact of new infrastructural developments on traffic, utilities, and overall city dynamics.

Research and Development:

In the realm of scientific research, AI is accelerating discoveries. Platforms like DeepMind's AlphaFold have made significant breakthroughs in protein folding predictions, a challenge that stumped scientists for decades. Such advancements have profound implications for understanding diseases and drug development.

Journalism and Media:

AI is making inroads into journalism, with tools like Heliograf by The Washington Post automating the generation of news articles, especially for data-intensive topics like sports or financial news. In media production, AI-driven software assists in video editing, optimizing content based on target audience preferences.

Legal Industry:

The legal profession, characterized by vast amounts of data, is ripe for AI intervention. Platforms like ROSS use AI to sift through legal documents, assisting lawyers in research. AI tools also predict legal outcomes based on historical data, aiding in strategy formulation.

Environmental Conservation:

AI is a potent tool in the fight against environmental challenges. Platforms like Orbital Insight use AI to analyze satellite imagery, tracking deforestation or illegal fishing activities in real-time. AI-driven climate models predict environmental changes, aiding policymakers in making informed decisions.

Having delved into the multifaceted influence of AI across a spectrum of industries, it becomes imperative to address its broader socio-economic implications. How does the rise of AI-driven methodologies impact employment patterns, job roles, and the very essence of work? The forthcoming section will navigate these intricate dynamics, shedding light on the opportunities and challenges presented by an AI-integrated job market.

AI's Impact on the Workforce

In the annals of human history, few technological advancements have promised or threatened (depending on one's perspective) to reshape the employment landscape as profoundly as artificial intelligence. As we stand at this pivotal juncture, it's crucial to understand that AI is not just another tool in our technological arsenal; it represents a paradigm shift in how we perceive, perform, and progress in our professional endeavors.

The integration of AI into the global economic fabric is both profound and pervasive. Its influence is not limited to automating mundane tasks or optimizing complex processes; it's about redefining roles, responsibilities, and relationships in the professional realm. From factory floors where robots collaborate with humans to design studios where AI algorithms assist in creative processes, the boundaries of what machines can achieve are continually expanding.

But what does this mean for the global workforce? On the one hand, there's palpable excitement. AI promises to eliminate repetitive tasks, offer intelligent insights, and even open up entirely new avenues of employment. On the other hand, there's apprehension. Stories of job displacements due to automation make headlines, fueling debates about the future of work in an AI-dominated landscape.

It's essential, however, to approach this topic with a balanced perspective. While AI does bring challenges, it also offers opportunities. The key lies in understanding, adapting, and evolving with this transformative force. As we delve deeper into this discussion, it's crucial to remember that every industrial revolution, from the advent of steam power to the rise of the internet, has brought its share of disruptions and opportunities. The AI revolution is no different.

Shift in Employment Patterns

The advent of artificial intelligence has ushered in a new era of employment dynamics. As AI systems become increasingly sophisticated and integrated into various industries, the patterns of employment are undergoing significant shifts. This transformation is not merely about job losses or gains; it's about the redistribution of roles across sectors, the evolution of job descriptions, and the emergence of entirely new professions.

At the heart of AI's impact on employment is its ability to automate tasks. However, it's crucial to understand that automation doesn't equate to job elimination universally. Instead, it often leads to job redistribution. For instance, while automation in the manufacturing sector might reduce the need for manual labor, it simultaneously increases the demand for technicians, programmers, and system maintainers who can oversee these automated systems.

The healthcare sector offers another illustrative example. While AI-driven diagnostic tools might reduce the time doctors spend on identifying diseases, they free up medical professionals to focus more on patient care, holistic treatment approaches, and complex medical procedures. Similarly, in the legal profession, while AI can sift through vast amounts of legal documentation rapidly, lawyers can dedicate more time to case strategies, client consultations, and courtroom presentations.

Growth vs. Reduction: A Sectoral Analysis

Certain industries are experiencing a pronounced growth in job opportunities due to AI. The tech sector, unsurprisingly, stands at the forefront. With the rise of AI, there's an escalating demand for data scientists, AI specialists, and machine learning engineers. These roles are pivotal in designing, refining, and implementing AI systems.

The education sector is also witnessing growth. With the integration of AI in educational tools and platforms, there's a rising demand for professionals who can bridge the gap between technology and pedagogy, crafting AI-driven educational experiences that are both effective and engaging.

Conversely, sectors heavily reliant on repetitive tasks face challenges. For instance, certain roles in the banking sector, like data entry or basic customer service, are being automated. Similarly, in the transportation industry, the rise of autonomous vehicles might, in the long run, impact jobs related to driving.

However, it's essential to approach these changes with nuance. Job reductions in one area often lead to growth in another within the same sector. Taking the transportation example further, while there might be fewer jobs for drivers in the future, there will be an increased demand for professionals skilled in autonomous vehicle technology, maintenance, and infrastructure development.

It's also worth noting that the timeline for these shifts varies. While some changes are already underway, others might unfold over decades, allowing the workforce ample time to adapt, reskill, and transition.

As we reflect on the shifting employment patterns, another intriguing facet of the AI revolution emerges: the birth of entirely new professions. While AI might be reshaping existing roles, it's also paving the way for jobs we hadn't envisioned a decade ago. So, what are these new roles? And how do they fit into the broader employment landscape? Let's delve into that topic.

Emergence of New Job Roles

The transformative power of artificial intelligence is not limited to reshaping existing professions; it's also catalyzing the birth of entirely new roles. As industries adapt to the capabilities of AI, the job market is expanding in directions previously uncharted, offering opportunities that blend technological prowess with domain-specific expertise.

Novel Professions Birthed by AI

AI Ethicist: As AI systems become integral to decision-making processes, there's a growing need for professionals who can ensure these systems operate within ethical boundaries. AI ethicists work at the intersection of technology and morality, crafting guidelines that ensure AI operates fairly, transparently, and without bias.

Chatbot Developer: With businesses increasingly relying on chatbots for customer service, there's a rising demand for professionals who can design, implement, and refine these virtual assistants, ensuring they provide accurate and human-like interactions.

AI Trainer: AI systems, especially those based on machine learning, require training. AI trainers work with these systems, feeding them data, refining their outputs, and ensuring they operate optimally. This role often requires domain-specific expertise, as trainers need to understand the context in which the AI operates.

Robotics Coordinator: In industries like healthcare and manufacturing, robots are becoming team members. Robotics coordinators ensure smooth human-robot collaboration, optimizing workflows and ensuring safety.

Data Detective: In an AI-driven world, anomalies in data can have significant implications. Data detectives delve into these anomalies, understanding their origins and implications, ensuring AI systems have accurate data to work with.

These roles, while nascent, highlight the diverse opportunities AI is introducing into the job market. They underscore the blend of technical and soft skills that will define the professions of the future.

Upskilling and Reskilling: Imperatives of the AI Era

The emergence of these new roles brings to the fore a critical aspect of the AI-driven job market: the need for continuous learning. As the boundaries of what AI can achieve expand, professionals must equip themselves with the skills to remain relevant.

Upskilling, or acquiring additional skills to excel in one's current role, becomes crucial. For instance, a financial analyst might upskill by learning to work with AI-driven data analysis tools, enhancing their analytical capabilities.

Reskilling, on the other hand, involves acquiring a new set of skills to transition to a different role. A factory worker, in the face of automation, might reskill to become a robot maintenance technician.

Educational institutions, businesses, and governments play pivotal roles in facilitating this upskilling and reskilling. Tailored courses, workshops, and training programs need to be designed, keeping in mind the evolving demands of the job market. Moreover, a culture of lifelong learning needs to be fostered, ensuring professionals view these transitions not as challenges but as opportunities for growth.

While the emergence of new roles paints an optimistic picture, concerns about AI leading to job displacement are prevalent. Are these concerns grounded in reality, or are they myths perpetuated by misunderstandings? We'll dissect the narratives surrounding AI and job displacement, separating fact from fiction and providing a balanced perspective on the future of work in the AI era.

The narrative surrounding artificial intelligence and its potential to displace jobs is as old as the concept of AI itself. As AI systems become increasingly integrated into various sectors, concerns about its impact on the workforce have amplified. But how much of this concern is based on reality, and how much is rooted in misconceptions? Let's delve into this intricate topic, separating myths from facts.

Misconceptions About AI and Mass Unemployment

One of the most pervasive myths is that AI will lead to mass unemployment. This belief stems from the idea that as machines become capable of performing tasks previously done by humans, there will be fewer jobs left for people. While it's undeniable that AI can automate certain tasks, equating automation with universal job loss is an oversimplification.

Historically, technological advancements have always led to shifts in the job market. The introduction of the printing press, the steam engine, and more recently, the internet, all led to concerns about job losses. However, in each instance, while certain jobs became obsolete, new ones emerged, often in greater numbers and requiring different skill sets.

Several studies have sought to understand the nuanced impact of AI on employment. According to a report by the World Economic Forum, while 75 million jobs might be displaced by AI and automation by 2022, 133 million new roles could emerge during the same period. This suggests a net gain in job opportunities.

Another study by McKinsey estimates that while up to 30% of tasks across 60% of jobs could be automated, fewer than 5% of jobs can be fully automated. This underscores the idea that AI will more often augment human roles rather than replace them entirely.

Furthermore, regions investing heavily in AI and automation, such as Scandinavia, have some of the lowest unemployment rates globally. This suggests that with the right policies and training programs in place, the integration of AI can lead to a thriving job market.

It's also worth noting that the nature of AI's impact varies across sectors. While roles in sectors like manufacturing might see a higher degree of automation, others, such as healthcare or education, will see AI augmenting human roles, leading to enhanced efficiency and new opportunities.

While AI's rise will undoubtedly lead to changes in the job market, framing it solely as a job displacer is a narrow perspective. AI, like any transformative technology, brings both challenges and opportunities. The key lies in understanding its nuanced impact, preparing the workforce for the changes, and leveraging

AI's capabilities to create a more inclusive, efficient, and innovative job market.

Having addressed the myths and realities surrounding AI and job displacement, it's essential to delve deeper into another facet of this transformation. How is AI influencing roles that have been foundational to industries for decades? As we navigate the next section, we'll explore how traditional professions are being reshaped, not replaced, by the advent of AI, offering a fresh perspective on the symbiotic relationship between humans and machines in the professional realm.

The Changing Nature of Traditional Roles

As we navigate the evolving landscape of artificial intelligence and its integration into the professional realm, it becomes evident that AI's influence is not about wholesale replacement as mentioned previously, but rather about augmentation and enhancement. Traditional roles, which have been the bedrock of various industries, are undergoing a metamorphosis, with AI acting as a catalyst for change.

The narrative of AI as a tool of replacement often overshadows its more profound role as an augmenter. In many professions, AI systems are not taking over entire job roles but are instead complementing human skills, leading to enhanced efficiency, accuracy, and innovation.

For instance, in the medical field, while AI-driven diagnostic tools can analyze medical images with remarkable precision, they don't replace radiologists. Instead, they assist them, reducing the chances of oversight and allowing radiologists to focus on more complex cases and patient interactions.

Similarly, in the realm of finance, while AI algorithms can analyze vast datasets to identify investment opportunities, they don't negate the need for human financial analysts. These professionals still play a pivotal role in interpreting data, understanding market nuances, and crafting strategies based on a blend of empirical data and human intuition.

Professions Transformed by AI Integration

Journalism: Tools like Heliograf by The Washington Post can automate the generation of news articles for data-intensive topics. However, journalists remain indispensable for in-depth reporting, interviews, and editorial pieces that require human touch, perspective, and judgment.

Architecture and Design: AI-driven design tools can suggest building layouts or product designs based on predefined parameters. Yet, architects and designers are crucial for infusing creativity, understanding client needs, and ensuring designs resonate with human aesthetics and emotions.

Teaching: While AI-driven platforms can offer personalized learning paths, teachers are essential for understanding student emotions, fostering classroom interactions, and instilling values and critical thinking skills.

Law Enforcement: AI tools can analyze vast amounts of data for patterns, aiding in investigations. However, police officers and detectives are vital for on-ground operations, understanding community dynamics, and making judgment calls in complex situations.

Sales and Marketing: AI can analyze consumer behavior and craft marketing strategies. Still, sales and marketing professionals are key for building relationships, understanding cultural nuances, and crafting narratives that resonate with diverse audiences.

These examples underscore a fundamental truth: AI is a tool that, when integrated thoughtfully, can elevate human potential. It doesn't diminish the value of human expertise but rather amplifies it, leading to outcomes that neither humans nor machines could achieve in isolation.

While the augmentation of traditional roles by AI offers a promising vista, it also brings forth a myriad of ethical considerations. How do we ensure that AI systems in the workplace operate fairly? What measures are in place to prevent biases in AI-driven hiring processes? As we transition to the next section, we'll delve into the ethical dimensions of AI in employment, exploring the challenges and the measures to address them in our quest for a just and inclusive AI-augmented professional landscape.

The Ethical Implications of AI in Employment

The integration of artificial intelligence into the employment sector, while promising a myriad of benefits, also raises profound ethical questions. As AI-driven systems play an increasingly pivotal role in hiring processes, performance evaluations, and more, concerns about fairness, bias, and transparency come to the fore. Addressing these concerns is not just a technological challenge but a moral imperative.

One of the most significant advantages of AI in hiring is its potential to analyze vast amounts of data rapidly, ensuring that the best candidates are shortlisted. However, this very strength can become a pitfall if not handled with care. AI systems, after all, are trained on data, and if this data carries historical biases, the AI can inadvertently perpetuate these biases.

For instance, if an AI-driven hiring tool is trained on data from an industry historically dominated by one gender, it might unintentionally favor candidates from that gender, sidelining equally or more qualified candidates from other genders. Similarly, biases related to ethnicity, age, or educational background can creep into AI systems if they're not explicitly addressed.

Transparency becomes crucial here. Companies using AI tools for hiring need to be open about how these tools work, the kind of data they're trained on, and the measures in place to ensure fairness. Candidates should have the right to know how decisions about their applications are being made, ensuring they're evaluated on merit and not sidelined due to algorithmic biases.

Given the profound implications of AI in employment, there's a growing consensus about the need for robust regulations and guidelines. These regulations aim to ensure that AI tools used in the job market adhere to ethical standards, prioritizing fairness and transparency.

Several countries and regions are already working on such guidelines. For instance, the European Union's

General Data Protection Regulation (GDPR) has provisions that relate to AI, ensuring that individuals have the right to know when automated decisions are being made about them.

Industry-specific guidelines are also emerging. Organizations are collaborating to craft best practices for AI in hiring, ensuring that these tools are used responsibly. These guidelines emphasize regular audits of AI systems, ensuring they remain free from biases and operate transparently.

Moreover, there's a growing emphasis on "explainable AI." This involves developing AI systems that not just make decisions but can also explain their decision-making processes in understandable terms. Such transparency is crucial in the employment sector, where decisions about hiring can profoundly impact individuals' lives.

Having navigated the ethical landscape of AI in employment, it's essential to look ahead. How can both employees and employers prepare for an AI-augmented future? What strategies can ensure a smooth transition, maximizing benefits while minimizing challenges? In the subsequent section, we'll offer recommendations tailored for both employees and employers, providing a roadmap for thriving in the AI-driven job market.

Preparing for the Future: Recommendations for Employees and Employers

As the wave of artificial intelligence continues to reshape the employment landscape, both employees and employers find themselves at a crossroads. The choices made today will determine the trajectory of the job market in the coming decades. To navigate this transformative era successfully, it's imperative to be proactive, informed, and adaptable. Here are some tailored recommendations for both employees and employers.

Strategies for Workers to Remain Relevant

Continuous Learning: In an ever-evolving technological landscape, the importance of lifelong learning cannot be overstated. Workers should actively seek out courses, workshops, and training programs that enhance their skills, especially in areas intersecting with AI.

Embrace Hybrid Roles: The future of work is likely to see roles that blend domain expertise with technological proficiency. For instance, a marketer who understands AI-driven analytics or a nurse adept at using AI-powered diagnostic tools will be invaluable.

Soft Skills Development: While AI excels at data-driven tasks, human-centric skills like empathy, communication, and creativity remain irreplaceable. Investing in developing these skills can ensure workers remain indispensable.

Networking: Engaging with professional communities, attending industry seminars, and participating in webinars can provide insights into the latest trends, ensuring workers are always a step ahead.

Recommendations for Employers

Transparent Communication: As AI systems are integrated into workplaces, it's crucial for employers to communicate these changes transparently. Employees should understand why these integrations are happening and how they'll impact their roles.

Reskilling Initiatives: Instead of looking externally for talent every time a new AI tool is adopted, employers should consider reskilling their current workforce. This not only saves recruitment costs but also boosts employee morale and loyalty.

Ethical AI Implementation: Employers should prioritize the ethical use of AI. This includes ensuring fairness in AI-driven decision-making processes and being transparent about how AI tools operate.

Collaborative Workspaces: The future workplace will likely see humans and AI systems working side by side. Designing workspaces that facilitate this collaboration can lead to enhanced efficiency and innovation.

Feedback Mechanisms: As AI tools are integrated, employers should establish feedback mechanisms, allowing employees to share their experiences, concerns, and suggestions regarding the AI systems. This feedback can be invaluable in refining and optimizing these tools.

Conclusion:

As we draw the curtains on our exploration of the economic impacts of artificial intelligence, it's evident that we are witnessing a transformative epoch in the annals of human history. The interplay between AI and the economic landscape is multifaceted, weaving together threads of opportunity, challenge, innovation, and ethical considerations.

Throughout this chapter, we've journeyed through the myriad ways AI is reshaping industries, from automation to the creation of entirely new sectors. We've grappled with the profound shifts in employment patterns, acknowledging both the fears of job displacement and the excitement of novel professions birthed by AI's rise. At every juncture, we've been reminded that while AI is a formidable force, its true potential is unlocked when it works in harmony with human ingenuity.

The ethical dimensions of AI in the workplace have underscored the importance of navigating this era with a compass guided by fairness, transparency, and inclusivity. As AI systems become more entrenched in hiring processes and performance evaluations, the onus is on us to ensure that these tools are wielded with responsibility and foresight.

Looking ahead, the trajectory of AI's economic impact is rife with potential. However, this potential is not preordained—it's shaped by the choices we make today. Policymakers, industry leaders, educators, and every individual have roles to play in crafting a future where AI doesn't just drive economic growth but does so in a manner that is equitable and beneficial for all.

In closing, the economic narrative of AI is still being written. It's a story of transformation, of challenges met with innovation, and of a future that promises a symphony of human and machine collaboration. As we continue our journey into subsequent chapters, we carry forward the insights gleaned from this exploration, ever mindful of the profound economic ripples AI is creating in its wake.

Chapter 4: AI in Daily Life

In the vast expanse of technological evolution, few innovations have permeated our daily lives as profoundly as artificial intelligence. From the moment we wake up, aided by a smart alarm that adjusts to our sleep cycle, to the evening when we ask a virtual assistant to play our favorite lullaby, AI is an omnipresent companion. This chapter delves into this intimate relationship between AI and our daily routines, exploring the myriad ways this technology enhances, simplifies, and sometimes complicates our everyday experiences.

Smart homes, virtual assistants, and personalized experiences

The concept of a 'home' has evolved dramatically with the advent of AI. No longer just a physical space, modern homes have transformed into interconnected ecosystems, where devices communicate seamlessly, driven by the power of AI.

The Rise of the Smart Home:

Imagine walking into your house after a long day at work. The lights adjust to a soft hue, your favorite playlist starts playing, and the thermostat sets itself to a cozy temperature. This isn't a scene from a sci-fi movie but the reality of many homes equipped with AI-driven smart systems. From smart thermostats that learn your preferences to security systems that can differentiate between a family member and an intruder, our homes are becoming more responsive and intuitive.

Virtual Assistants - The Digital Companions:

"Hey Siri, what's the weather like today?" or "Alexa, set a timer for 10 minutes." Phrases like these have become commonplace. Virtual assistants, powered by sophisticated AI algorithms, have become our personal aides, helping us with tasks ranging from setting reminders to answering trivia. Their ability to understand natural language, combined with machine learning, allows them to continuously evolve, becoming more attuned to our preferences and habits.

Personalized Experiences in a Digital World:

AI's influence isn't limited to smart homes or virtual assistants. It extends to the digital platforms we interact with daily. Streaming services like Netflix or Spotify use AI to analyze our viewing or listening habits, offering recommendations tailored to our tastes. Online shopping platforms employ AI to showcase products we're more likely to purchase, based on our browsing history and past purchases.

These personalized experiences, while enhancing convenience, also raise questions about privacy and the amount of data we're willing to share. As AI systems become more integrated into our daily routines, striking a balance between personalization and privacy will be pivotal.

While the broader applications of AI in our daily lives paint a picture of technological marvel, diving deep into specific instances offers a more nuanced understanding. One such instance that has left an indelible mark on the world of AI and daily life is the evolution of Apple's voice assistant, Siri.

Case Study: The Evolution of Siri – From App to Apple's Voice

In the realm of virtual assistants, Siri stands as a testament to the transformative power of AI in our daily lives. Its journey, from a standalone app to becoming an integral voice of Apple's ecosystem, offers a fascinating glimpse into the rapid evolution of AI-driven technologies.

Siri's story began in 2007, not as a brainchild of Apple, but as a project funded by the Defense Advanced Research Projects Agency (DARPA). The initial goal was ambitious: to create a virtual assistant that could assist military personnel in their tasks. By 2010, Siri had evolved into a standalone app available on the App Store, promising iPhone users the ability to "send messages, place phone calls, and more" using just their voice.

Recognizing the potential of Siri, Apple acquired the technology in 2010. A year later, with the launch of the iPhone 4S, Siri was introduced as a built-in feature, marking a significant shift in how users interacted with their devices. No longer was voice recognition just about simple commands; Siri could understand context, answer questions, set reminders, and even crack a joke or two.

Over the years, Siri has undergone numerous updates, each enhancing its capabilities. From understanding multiple languages to integrating with third-party apps, Siri's growth mirrored the broader advancements in AI. Features like 'Shortcuts' allowed users to create custom voice commands, further personalizing their experience.

One of the standout evolutions was Siri's ability to operate across devices. Whether you're using an iPhone, iPad, Apple Watch, or even the HomePod, Siri's presence ensured a seamless experience.

Challenges and Criticisms:

Siri's journey hasn't been without challenges. Competing voice assistants like Amazon's Alexa and Google Assistant pushed the boundaries of what users expected from their virtual aides. Siri faced criticisms over issues like voice recognition accuracy and the breadth of its knowledge base.

However, Apple's continuous investments in AI and machine learning have ensured that Siri remains at the forefront of virtual assistant technology, addressing these challenges head-on.

The Broader Impact:

Siri's significance extends beyond its technical capabilities. It changed perceptions. Voice-driven interactions, once a novelty, became mainstream, setting the stage for a new era of human-computer interaction. Siri's widespread recognition also paved the way for the acceptance and adoption of other AI-driven virtual assistants.

While Siri offers a compelling narrative of AI's integration into personal devices, the influence of artificial intelligence doesn't stop there. Its ripples are felt across various sectors, from the movies we watch to the way we learn and even how we monitor our health. As we transition from the personal realm of virtual assistants, let's delve into the broader applications of AI in entertainment, healthcare, and education, and uncover the profound ways it's reshaping these domains.

The Role of AI in Entertainment, Healthcare, and Education

The entertainment industry has always been at the forefront of technological innovation, and with AI, it's no different. Today, AI plays a pivotal role in content creation, distribution, and consumption.

Content Recommendation: As mentioned earlier platforms like Netflix and Spotify use AI-driven algorithms to analyze user preferences and behavior, offering tailored content recommendations. This personalization enhances user engagement and ensures a more satisfying user experience.

Content Creation: AI tools assist in movie production, from scriptwriting to post-production effects. For instance, AI algorithms can analyze vast amounts of data to predict which movie plots might be hits or misses.

Gaming: Video games now employ AI to create more challenging and adaptive opponents, enhancing gameplay. Games like 'The Last of Us Part II' have showcased advanced AI-driven characters that react more realistically to player actions.

Healthcare: Revolutionizing Patient Care

AI's impact on healthcare is profound, promising to revolutionize patient care, diagnostics, and treatment.

Diagnostics: AI-driven tools, like Google's DeepMind, have shown the ability to detect diseases such as diabetic retinopathy and age-related macular degeneration by analyzing eye scans.

Treatment Personalization: AI algorithms analyze patient data to recommend personalized treatment plans, considering factors like genetics and lifestyle.

Drug Discovery: Traditional drug discovery processes are time-consuming and expensive. AI expedites this by analyzing complex biochemical interactions. Atomwise is a notable example, using AI for drug discovery, reducing both time and costs.

Education: Personalized Learning and Beyond

The realm of education is undergoing a seismic shift with the integration of AI, moving towards more personalized and efficient learning experiences.

Adaptive Learning Platforms: AI-driven platforms adjust content in real-time based on a student's performance, ensuring they're always challenged at the right level.

Administrative Tasks: AI tools help automate administrative tasks for educators, like grading assignments, allowing them to spend more time on instruction.

Tutoring Systems: AI-driven tutoring systems provide students with personalized assistance outside of classroom hours, ensuring they get help precisely when they need it.

While these broad strokes paint a picture of AI's transformative impact across sectors, it's in the detailed narratives of specific instances that we truly grasp its depth and breadth. Through the lens of case studies, we can delve deeper, understanding not just the 'how' but also the 'why' behind AI's role in these domains. Let's embark on this deeper exploration, starting with the entertainment sector, where AI's influence has redefined content consumption paradigms.

Case Study: AI in Entertainment - "StreamTech's AI-Powered Content Recommendation System"

In the vast landscape of digital entertainment, content is king. But with millions of hours of content available, how do platforms ensure that viewers find what they love? Enter StreamTech, a leading streaming platform, and its groundbreaking AI-powered content recommendation system.

With a diverse user base spanning ages, cultures, and preferences, StreamTech faced a challenge: How to offer personalized content recommendations that keep users engaged and subscribed?

StreamTech developed an advanced AI algorithm that analyzed multiple data points: viewing history, search queries, watch durations, and even pauses or rewinds. But it didn't stop there. The system also factored in broader trends, analyzing global viewing patterns and seasonal preferences.

One of StreamTech's standout features was its real-time adaptability. If a user started watching more of a particular genre, the system would immediately adjust, offering recommendations from that genre in subsequent viewing sessions.

The results were staggering. User engagement shot up by 40%, and subscription churn rates dropped significantly. More users reported finding their "new favorite show" on StreamTech, a testament to the system's accuracy.

While the AI-driven recommendation system was a game-changer, it wasn't without challenges. Concerns about data privacy emerged, with users questioning how their viewing data was being used. StreamTech responded by offering more transparent user controls and clearer data usage policies.

Looking ahead, StreamTech plans to integrate voice recognition, allowing users to ask for recommendations vocally, making the user experience even more seamless and interactive.

While StreamTech's story underscores AI's transformative potential in entertainment, its impact isn't limited to our screens. In the realm of healthcare, AI is ushering in a new era of diagnostics and treatment, promising better outcomes and more efficient care.

Case Study: AI in Healthcare - "MediBot: Revolutionizing Diagnostics with AI"

The healthcare sector, with its vast data repositories and critical decision-making, stands as a prime candidate for AI-driven transformation. Among the myriad innovations, MediBot emerges as a beacon, showcasing the potential of AI in diagnostics.

MediBot was conceived in a leading tech-healthcare collaborative initiative in 2019. The vision was clear: to develop an AI-driven diagnostic tool that could assist doctors in making accurate, timely, and efficient diagnoses.

How MediBot Works:

Harnessing the power of deep learning, MediBot analyzes patient symptoms, medical history, and even genomic data. It then cross-references this information with vast medical databases, research papers, and clinical studies to provide potential diagnoses.

In preliminary tests, MediBot showcased an accuracy rate of over 90% in diagnosing a range of conditions, from common ailments to rare diseases. Its ability to quickly sift through vast amounts of data meant that diagnoses were often made in a fraction of the traditional time.

While MediBot's capabilities are impressive, it's designed to be a tool for healthcare professionals, not a replacement. Doctors use MediBot's insights as a reference, combining it with their expertise to make informed decisions.

Like all AI-driven tools, MediBot faces challenges. Ensuring data privacy, managing the vast and ever-growing medical databases, and continuous training to keep the AI updated are ongoing tasks. However, with the promise of transforming patient care and potentially saving countless lives, the journey forward is filled with optimism.

The transformative power of AI, as seen with MediBot in healthcare, extends its reach into the classrooms and lecture halls of our educational institutions. As we transition from the realm of healthcare, let's explore how AI is reshaping the educational landscape, offering personalized and efficient learning experiences.

Case Study: AI in Education - "EduTech AI: Personalized Learning Platforms"

Education, a cornerstone of societal advancement, has often been constrained by a one-size-fits-all approach. However, with the advent of AI, platforms like EduTech AI are challenging this norm, offering tailored learning experiences that cater to individual needs.

Founded in 2017, EduTech AI sought to address a fundamental challenge in education: How can learning be made more personal and adaptive? The answer lay in harnessing the power of AI to create dynamic learning platforms.

How EduTech AI Works:

Upon enrollment, students undergo an initial assessment. The AI system analyzes their strengths, weaknesses, preferences, and pace. Based on this data, a customized learning path is crafted for each student.

As students progress, the system continuously monitors their performance, adjusting the learning materials in real-time. For instance, if a student struggles with algebra but excels in geometry, the platform might integrate more visual and spatial exercises into their algebra lessons.

Beyond Academics:

EduTech AI's platform isn't just about academic subjects. It also offers modules on life skills, emotional intelligence, and other essential competencies, ensuring a holistic education.

In a pilot program conducted in 2019, schools that integrated EduTech AI reported a 35% increase in overall student performance. Furthermore, students reported higher engagement levels, with 80% stating that they felt more in control of their learning journey.

While the results are promising, challenges like ensuring data privacy, training teachers to use the platform effectively, and making the technology accessible to students from all socio-economic backgrounds remain. However, with continuous refinements and collaborations with educational institutions, EduTech AI aims to make personalized learning the norm rather than the exception.

Conclusion

As we journeyed through the realms of entertainment, healthcare, and education, the pervasive influence of AI became evident. From the way we consume content to how we diagnose illnesses and tailor educational experiences, AI's footprint is undeniable.

Yet, as with all technological advancements, it's essential to approach AI with a balanced perspective. While it offers unprecedented conveniences and efficiencies, challenges around data privacy, ethical considerations, and the human touch remain.

The narratives of StreamTech, MediBot, and EduTech AI serve as microcosms of the broader AI landscape. They underscore the potential, the challenges, and the continuous evolution that defines AI's role in our daily lives.

As we conclude this chapter, it's evident that AI isn't just a technological marvel; it's an integral part of our daily tapestry, shaping, enhancing, and sometimes challenging our everyday experiences.

Chapter 5: Ethical Implications of AI

In the age of rapid technological advancements, artificial intelligence stands out as one of the most transformative forces. Its capabilities, from automating mundane tasks to making complex decisions, have heralded a new era of convenience and efficiency. However, with this power comes a myriad of ethical dilemmas that challenge our traditional norms and values.

The rise of AI has brought forth questions that were once the domain of philosophical debates but are now pressing practical concerns. Who is responsible when an AI makes a mistake? How do we ensure that these systems don't perpetuate or even exacerbate societal biases? And perhaps most prominently, in an age where data is the new oil, how do we safeguard individual privacy?

These concerns aren't just theoretical. Real-world incidents, from data breaches to controversial AI-driven decisions, have underscored the urgency of addressing these ethical challenges. As we stand on the cusp of an AI-driven future, it's imperative to navigate these murky waters with a keen sense of responsibility and foresight.

Understanding the ethical implications of AI isn't just about preventing mishaps; it's about ensuring that as we integrate AI more deeply into our societies, we do so in a manner that aligns with our shared values and ideals. It's about striking a balance between innovation and ethics, ensuring that the AI-driven future is one that we can all look forward to with optimism and trust.

While the broader ethical landscape of AI presents a myriad of challenges, one concern stands out due to its immediate relevance and potential consequences: the issue of privacy. In a world where our every click, like, and share is tracked, how does AI play into the evolving dynamics of data privacy and security? Let's delve deeper into this pressing concern.

Privacy Concerns and Data Security

In today's digital age, data has become an invaluable asset. Every online interaction, transaction, and behavior generates data, which, when harnessed correctly, can offer unparalleled insights and personalization. However, this vast reservoir of data also brings with it significant concerns, especially in the realm of privacy and security.

Data, in its essence, is neutral. It's how it's used that defines its value or risk. On one hand, data-driven insights have led to remarkable advancements. Think of the personalized movie recommendations on streaming platforms or targeted advertisements that seem to know just what you're looking for. These conveniences are powered by complex AI algorithms that analyze vast amounts of user data to predict preferences and behaviors.

However, the other side of this coin is darker. The same data that enables personalization can be misused, leading to breaches of privacy. Personal information can be sold to third parties, used to manipulate user behavior, or even exploited for more nefarious purposes.

The Role of AI in Data Collection, Analysis, and Potential Breaches

Artificial Intelligence amplifies the capabilities of data processing. Traditional data analysis methods, which relied on manual input and were constrained by human limitations, are now being overshadowed by AI's ability to process and analyze vast datasets in real-time.

But with this capability comes responsibility. AI systems, if not designed with robust security measures, can become vulnerable to breaches. Hackers, recognizing the value of data, are increasingly targeting AI-driven platforms. Moreover, AI can be used to identify potential vulnerabilities in other systems, making the cybersecurity landscape even more complex.

The crux of the matter lies in finding a balance. As consumers, we crave the conveniences that personalized services offer. Yet, we also want to ensure that our personal data remains secure. The challenge for businesses and developers is to innovate while also ensuring robust data protection measures.

Regulations like the General Data Protection Regulation (GDPR) in Europe have set stringent standards for data protection, emphasizing user consent and transparency. Such regulations push companies to be more responsible, but they also pose challenges, especially for AI-driven services that rely heavily on user data.

The future, therefore, lies in developing AI systems that are not only intelligent but also ethical. Transparent algorithms, robust security measures, and a commitment to user privacy will be the pillars of future AI innovations.

While the theoretical discussions around data privacy are essential, real-world incidents bring these concerns to life, highlighting the tangible consequences of data misuse. One such incident that shook the world and brought the ethical implications of data and AI to the forefront was the Cambridge Analytica scandal. Let's delve into this case to understand the intricate interplay between data, democracy, and AI.

Case Study: The Cambridge Analytica Scandal – Data, Democracy, and AI

In the annals of data breaches and misuse, few incidents have garnered as much attention and scrutiny as the Cambridge Analytica scandal. It wasn't just about data; it was about the very fabric of democracy and how susceptible it could be to manipulation in the age of AI.

Cambridge Analytica, a political consulting firm, accessed the data of millions of Facebook users without their explicit consent. But the breach wasn't just about accessing data; it was about how that data was used. The firm aimed to influence voter behavior in various elections, most notably the 2016 U.S. Presidential Election.

Using a seemingly innocuous quiz app, the firm was able to gather not just the data of those who took the quiz but also that of their friends, amassing a treasure trove of information on millions. This data included likes, shares, and even private messages, painting a detailed picture of individual users.

With this vast amount of data in hand, simple data analytics wouldn't suffice. Cambridge Analytica employed sophisticated AI algorithms to analyze and segment the data. The goal? To create detailed psychological profiles of users, categorizing them based on their susceptibilities and inclinations.

These profiles enabled highly targeted political advertising. Messages were crafted to resonate with specific segments, playing on their fears, aspirations, and beliefs. It was psychological manipulation on an unprecedented scale, made possible by the combined power of data and AI.

The revelation of the scandal sent shockwaves around the world. It raised pressing questions about data privacy, consent, and the ethical use of AI. Facebook faced intense scrutiny, with its CEO, Mark Zuckerberg, testifying before Congress. The incident led to calls for stricter data protection regulations and a more transparent use of AI in political campaigns.

Cambridge Analytica closed its operations, but the lessons from the scandal remain. It underscored the need for tech companies to be more responsible stewards of user data and for users to be more aware of how their data can be used, and potentially misused.

While the Cambridge Analytica scandal highlighted the potential misuse of data in the political realm, it's essential to recognize that ethical concerns with AI aren't limited to data privacy. Another pressing issue in the AI community is the potential for bias in AI algorithms. How do we ensure that these systems, which are increasingly influencing critical decisions, are fair and unbiased? Let's explore the challenges and potential solutions in ensuring bias and fairness in AI algorithms.

Bias and Fairness in AI Algorithms

Artificial Intelligence, for all its computational prowess, is not immune to the biases that permeate human society. These biases, when left unchecked, can manifest in AI systems, leading to skewed results and perpetuating existing inequalities.

At its core, AI learns from data. If this data carries biases, the AI system will inevitably inherit them. For instance, if an AI model is trained on historical hiring data from a company that has predominantly favored a particular gender or ethnicity, the model might perpetuate that bias, favoring similar candidates in the future.

But it's not just about the data. The very individuals who design and train AI models come with their own set of biases. If these biases influence decisions about which data to include or exclude, or how to structure the model, the AI system can become skewed.

The implications of biased AI are vast and varied:

Hiring Processes: As companies increasingly rely on AI-driven tools for recruitment, there's a risk that these tools might favor or exclude candidates based on gender, ethnicity, or other irrelevant factors, leading to a lack of diversity and potential legal implications.

Criminal Sentencing: Some jurisdictions have started using AI tools to assess the risk of reoffending among convicts. If these tools are biased, they might disproportionately label certain groups as high-risk, leading to longer sentences or denied parole.

Credit and Loan Approvals: AI-driven credit scoring can inadvertently disadvantage certain demographics if the models are trained on biased data, leading to denied loans or higher interest rates.

Strategies to Mitigate and Prevent AI Bias

Diverse Training Data: Ensuring that the data used to train AI models is representative of diverse groups can help in reducing bias. This might involve sourcing data from varied demographics or even synthetically creating data to balance out disparities.

Transparency and Explainability: If AI models can explain their decisions, it becomes easier to identify and rectify biases. Transparent AI models allow for scrutiny and validation by third parties.

Regular Audits: Periodic reviews of AI systems, especially those used in critical decision-making, can help in identifying and rectifying biases. These audits can be conducted by internal teams or third-party experts.

Ethical Guidelines: Establishing a set of ethical guidelines for AI development can serve as a roadmap for developers, ensuring that they consider potential biases at every stage of the development process.

While understanding and addressing biases in AI is crucial, real-world case studies often offer the most profound insights. One such area where AI's potential bias has garnered significant attention is in hiring. As companies increasingly turn to AI to streamline their recruitment processes, how do we ensure fairness and avoid perpetuating existing biases? Let's delve into a case study that highlights the challenges and potential solutions in AI-driven hiring.

Case Study: AI in Hiring - The Bias Dilemma

The promise of AI in recruitment is undeniable: faster processes, reduced human error, and the ability to analyze vast amounts of data to find the perfect candidate. However, as with many AI applications, the potential for bias lurks in the shadows.

One of the most prominent instances came to light when a tech giant's AI recruitment tool was found to be biased against female candidates. The tool, designed to review resumes and shortlist candidates, was trained on a decade's worth of resumes submitted to the company. Given the tech industry's male-dominated nature, the majority of these resumes were from men. The AI, learning from this data, began to favor male candidates. Resumes that included words like "women's chess club captain" or had names of all-women's colleges were ranked lower by the system.

But it's not an isolated incident. Other AI-driven hiring tools have been found to favor candidates based on factors like age, ethnicity, or even socioeconomic status, leading to concerns about the perpetuation of existing inequalities in the job market.

The revelation of biases in AI recruitment tools led to significant backlash. Companies faced criticism, not just for the biased outcomes but also for their over-reliance on AI without adequate checks and balances.

In response, many organizations began to reevaluate their AI recruitment strategies. The tech giant scrapped its biased tool, but the incident served as a wake-up call for the industry. Companies started investing in more transparent AI models, allowing for greater scrutiny of their decision-making processes. There was also a push for more diverse training data to ensure that AI models had a more balanced foundation to learn from.

Moreover, the incident highlighted the importance of human oversight in AI-driven processes. While AI can assist in sifting through vast amounts of data, the final decision, many argue, should always involve human judgment.

The road to unbiased AI recruitment is ongoing. It involves a combination of better data, more transparent algorithms, and a commitment to continuous learning and improvement. The goal is clear: harness the power of AI to make hiring more efficient without compromising on fairness and equality.

The challenges posed by biases in AI-driven hiring tools underscore a broader issue in the realm of AI ethics: the need for transparency and accountability. As AI systems become more integrated into critical decision-making processes, how do we ensure that they are not just smart, but also transparent, accountable, and regulated? Let's delve deeper into these essential facets of ethical AI.

Transparency, Accountability, and Regulation

As AI systems become increasingly sophisticated, their decision-making processes can become more opaque. This complexity, while a testament to the advancements in the field, also poses challenges, especially when these systems influence critical areas of our lives, from healthcare to finance.

One of the most significant challenges in modern AI is the "black box" problem. Many advanced AI models, especially deep learning systems, make decisions based on complex computations that are not easily interpretable by humans. While these models can achieve remarkable accuracy, their lack of transparency can be problematic.

Imagine a scenario where an AI system denies a loan application or flags someone as a high medical risk but cannot explain why. Such situations can lead to mistrust and skepticism, not to mention potential legal and ethical issues. For AI to be widely accepted and integrated, especially in critical decision-making areas, its decisions must be explainable and justifiable.

Holding AI Developers and Users Accountable for Their Systems

Accountability in AI goes beyond just the algorithms. It extends to those who design, deploy, and use these systems. If an AI system makes a mistake or causes harm, who is responsible? The developer? The user? The organization deploying it?

Clear lines of accountability are essential to ensure that AI systems are used responsibly. This involves setting standards for AI development, ensuring rigorous testing before deployment, and establishing protocols for when things go wrong.

Moreover, accountability also means that AI developers and companies are responsible for continuously updating and refining their systems, especially as new data becomes available or as societal norms and values evolve.

Given the profound impact of AI on society, there's a growing consensus that the field needs regulation. However, regulating AI is not straightforward. The technology evolves rapidly, and regulations need to strike a balance between fostering innovation and ensuring safety and ethics.

Several countries and regions have started drafting AI guidelines and regulations. For instance, as the European Union's General Data Protection Regulation (GDPR) includes provisions related to AI and automated decision-making. Similarly, various industry groups and AI researchers are working on ethical guidelines for AI development.

These regulations and guidelines aim to ensure that AI systems respect user rights, are transparent in their operations, and are accountable for their decisions. They also emphasize the importance of fairness, ensuring that AI does not perpetuate or exacerbate societal biases.

While the broader discussions around AI transparency and accountability are essential, real-world case studies often offer the most profound insights. In the realm of healthcare, where decisions can be a matter of life and death, how do we ensure that AI systems are not just accurate but also transparent? Let's explore this challenge through a case study that delves into the intricacies of AI-driven diagnoses.

Case Study: AI in Healthcare - The Transparent Diagnosis Challenge

Healthcare, with its vast datasets and the critical nature of its decisions, is a prime candidate for AI integration.

From predicting patient deterioration to diagnosing diseases from medical images, AI has shown immense promise. However, with this potential comes a unique set of challenges, especially concerning transparency.

AI-driven diagnostic tools, especially those based on deep learning, have achieved remarkable accuracy rates. For instance, certain AI models can detect specific cancers in medical images with an accuracy comparable to, or even surpassing, human experts. But how these models arrive at their conclusions remains largely inscrutable.

In a field like healthcare, where decisions can have life-altering consequences, the "trust" factor is paramount. A radiologist using an AI tool to aid in diagnosis would want to understand why the AI flagged a particular region in an image. Similarly, patients, when informed of a diagnosis made with the assistance of AI, might want clarity on how that conclusion was reached.

In healthcare, both human experts and AI systems are susceptible to errors. A misdiagnosis, regardless of its origin, can result in inappropriate treatments and potential harm to the patient. When an AI system errs, the immediate concern is the patient's well-being. Beyond that, such mistakes can erode trust in AI-driven healthcare tools. High-profile errors, in particular, can foster skepticism, hindering the adoption and progress of these advanced tools in the field.

Steps Taken to Ensure Clarity and Trust in AI Healthcare Tools

Recognizing the challenges, researchers, and industry leaders have been working on multiple fronts to enhance the transparency and trustworthiness of AI in healthcare:

- **Explainable AI (XAI):** Efforts are underway to develop AI models that, while retaining their accuracy, can provide insights into their decision-making processes. These models might highlight critical regions in an image or provide a confidence score along with their diagnosis.

- **Robust Testing:** Before deployment, AI models undergo rigorous testing, often on diverse datasets, to ensure their accuracy and reliability. This testing can help in identifying potential biases or blind spots in the models.

- **Human-AI Collaboration:** Many in the field advocate for a collaborative approach, where AI tools serve as assistants to human experts rather than replacements. In such a setup, the AI system provides its insights, but the final decision rests with the human expert, combining the computational prowess of AI with the experience and intuition of professionals.

- **Feedback Loops:** Some AI systems are designed with feedback mechanisms, allowing users to provide feedback on the tool's decisions. This feedback can be used to refine and improve the model over time.

The integration of AI in healthcare is a journey filled with promise but also challenges. As we navigate this path, the focus must remain on ensuring that these tools, while powerful, are transparent, trustworthy, and always in service of patient care.

Conclusion:

As we've journeyed through the ethical dimensions of artificial intelligence, it's evident that the integration of AI into our daily lives and critical sectors is not without its challenges. From the intricacies of data privacy to the nuances of algorithmic bias, the ethical landscape of AI is as vast as it is complex.

The case studies presented, from the misuse of data in political campaigns to the challenges of transparency in healthcare diagnostics, underscore the real-world implications of these ethical dilemmas. They serve as reminders that while AI holds immense promise, it also bears significant responsibilities.

However, it's heartening to see the proactive steps being taken by researchers, policymakers, and industry leaders. The development of explainable AI models, the drafting of comprehensive regulations, and the emphasis on human-AI collaboration are all testament to a collective commitment to ethical AI.

As we look forward to the continued evolution of AI, one thing is clear: the conversation around its ethical implications is not a mere footnote but a central narrative. It's a dialogue that requires the active participation of all stakeholders, from developers to end-users, to ensure that as AI reshapes our world, it does so in a manner that is transparent, fair, and aligned with our shared values.

Chapter 6: The Societal Shift: AI's Broader Impacts

Artificial Intelligence stands out as one of the most impactful technological developments in our history. As we navigate through this evolving era, AI seamlessly integrates into our everyday lives, significantly shaping not only our industries and economies but also altering the dynamics of our societal interactions and structures.

From the way we forge personal connections to how we perceive and interact with the world at large, AI acts as both a lens and a mirror. It reflects our biases, aspirations, and desires while simultaneously shaping our experiences based on vast datasets and complex algorithms.

This chapter delves deep into the societal shifts brought about by AI. We'll explore the nuances of our AI-augmented personal relationships, understand its role in our professional lives, and even traverse the global landscape to witness AI's influence across different cultures and societies. Through real-world case studies, we'll also confront some of the ethical dilemmas posed by this transformative technology.

As we embark on this exploration, let's begin by understanding how AI has influenced our personal relationships in the age of social media, dating apps, and digital communication.

AI and Personal Relationships

In today's digital age, our social connections are increasingly mediated by technology. From the friends we make to the news we consume, algorithms play a pivotal role in shaping our social experiences. Artificial Intelligence, with its ability to analyze vast amounts of data and predict user preferences, has become a cornerstone of this digital social landscape.

How AI-Driven Platforms Influence Our Social Connections

Social media platforms, driven by sophisticated AI algorithms, have transformed the way we connect, communicate, and even perceive the world around us. These platforms use AI to curate content, ensuring that our feeds are filled with posts, news, and advertisements tailored to our preferences. While this personalization can enhance user experience by providing relevant content, it also has its drawbacks.

The AI-driven personalization can sometimes create "echo chambers" or "filter bubbles," where users are only exposed to information that aligns with their existing beliefs. This can limit our exposure to diverse perspectives and can even polarize opinions on contentious topics. For instance, two individuals with differing political views might receive entirely different news updates on the same event, each tailored to reinforce their pre-existing beliefs.

Moreover, AI-driven recommendation systems on platforms like YouTube or TikTok can lead users down rabbit holes, where one video leads to another, keeping users engaged, sometimes at the cost of accurate information.

Beyond social media, AI has also reshaped the realm of personal relationships through dating apps. Platforms like Tinder, Bumble, and eHarmony use AI algorithms to suggest potential matches based on user preferences, behaviors, and even conversation styles. These algorithms analyze user data, from the photos they like to the bios they write, to predict potential compatibility.

While many have found meaningful connections through these platforms, the AI-driven nature of these apps also raises questions. Is love truly quantifiable? Can an algorithm determine compatibility? Some critics argue that while AI can predict superficial compatibility based on likes and dislikes, the deeper nuances of human relationships might be beyond its grasp.

Furthermore, AI-driven friend suggestion features on platforms like Facebook have enabled users to connect with long-lost friends or even distant relatives. These algorithms analyze mutual connections, shared activities, and other data points to suggest potential friends.

While AI's influence on personal relationships is profound, its impact doesn't stop at our personal lives. In the professional realm, AI is reshaping how we collaborate, communicate, and even conduct business. Let's explore how AI is transforming our professional interactions.

AI in Professional Interactions

In the realm of professional interactions, Artificial Intelligence has emerged as a game-changer. Its influence is palpable, from the boardrooms of multinational corporations to the dynamic startups in Silicon Valley and beyond.

The modern workplace is undergoing a significant transformation, driven in large part by AI. Tasks that once required hours of manual labor are now automated, leading to increased efficiency and productivity. For instance, AI-driven customer service bots can handle routine queries, freeing up human agents to tackle more complex issues. Similarly, advanced data analytics tools powered by AI can sift through vast amounts of data, providing businesses with actionable insights in real-time.

Beyond task automation, AI is also enhancing decision-making processes. Predictive analytics, for example, allows businesses to forecast market trends, helping them stay ahead of the curve. Furthermore, AI-driven collaboration tools are making project management more streamlined, with algorithms that can prioritize tasks, allocate resources, and even predict potential roadblocks.

AI's Role in Remote Work and Global Collaborations

The recent global events have underscored the importance of remote work, and AI has played a pivotal role in facilitating this shift. Virtual assistants, powered by AI, help manage schedules, set up meetings, and even provide real-time transcription services. Moreover, AI-driven communication platforms optimize video and audio quality in real-time, ensuring smooth virtual meetings irrespective of bandwidth constraints.

In the realm of global collaborations, AI is bridging the gap between teams spread across different geographies. Translation tools, backed by sophisticated AI algorithms, ensure that language is no longer a barrier. Additionally, AI-driven project management tools can account for different time zones, ensuring that teams worldwide can collaborate seamlessly.

While AI's influence in reshaping professional interactions is profound, its impact extends beyond the confines of the workplace. As we venture further, we'll explore how AI is playing a pivotal role in the broader context of global governance, shaping policies, regulations, and the very dynamics of international relations.

AI's Role in Global Governance

As nations grapple with the rapid advancements in Artificial Intelligence, its implications for global governance are becoming increasingly evident. From public policy to international relations, AI is both a tool and a challenge for governments worldwide.

Different nations have adopted varied stances towards AI, reflecting their unique socio-political contexts and technological aspirations. For instance:

- **The United States** has been a hub for AI innovation, with Silicon Valley leading the charge. The government's approach has largely been to foster innovation while ensuring that there are checks and balances in place. Regulatory bodies like the Federal Trade Commission (FTC) have issued guidelines on AI usage, especially concerning fairness and transparency.

- **India** is emerging as a significant player in the AI landscape, driven by its vast IT talent pool and burgeoning startup ecosystem. The government has recognized AI's potential to address some of the country's unique challenges, from healthcare to agriculture. Initiatives like the National Strategy for Artificial Intelligence outline India's vision to leverage AI for inclusive growth. However, with this push towards AI adoption, there are also growing concerns about data privacy and the need for a robust regulatory framework. The Personal Data Protection Bill, currently under discussion, aims to address some of these concerns, drawing inspiration from global standards while catering to India's specific needs.

- **China**, on the other hand, sees AI as a strategic tool for both economic growth and governance. The government has rolled out ambitious plans to become a global leader in AI by 2030. However, this aggressive push for AI supremacy also raises concerns about surveillance and individual rights.

Across the board, the challenge for governments is to strike a balance: fostering innovation while ensuring that the technology is used ethically and responsibly.

The Balance Between AI-Driven Surveillance and Citizen Privacy

One of the most contentious issues in the realm of AI and governance is surveillance. AI-driven surveillance tools, from facial recognition systems to predictive policing algorithms, offer governments unprecedented capabilities to monitor and control populations.

While these tools can enhance security and law enforcement, they also pose significant threats to individual privacy and civil liberties. In nations with authoritarian regimes, there's a growing concern that AI could be used to stifle dissent and tighten political control.

However, even in democracies, the unchecked use of AI surveillance tools can lead to overreach. The challenge, therefore, is to ensure that while governments leverage AI for security, they do so without compromising the fundamental rights of their citizens.

Having explored the intricate dance between AI and global governance, it's evident that the technology's influence isn't limited to the corridors of power. Its ripples are felt across various facets of society, from how we learn to how we trade. Let's delve deeper into AI's role in reshaping education and commerce across different cultures and regions.

AI in Education and Commerce Across Cultures

The transformative power of Artificial Intelligence isn't confined to any single region or culture. Its influence spans the globe, reshaping sectors as foundational as education and commerce. However, the way AI is integrated and its subsequent impact can vary significantly based on cultural, economic, and societal contexts.

Education, a cornerstone of societal advancement, is undergoing a revolution with the infusion of AI. In developed nations, AI-driven personalized learning platforms are becoming the norm. These tools assess individual student strengths, weaknesses, preferences, and pacing, delivering tailored educational content. For instance, in countries like the U.S. and parts of Europe, tools like Khan Academy and Coursera use AI to customize learning paths for students.

Contrastingly, in developing regions, AI's role in education often focuses on accessibility and outreach. For instance, in parts of Africa, AI-driven apps are being used to deliver basic education in regions where traditional schooling is a challenge due to infrastructural or geopolitical reasons.

How Commerce and Trade are Being Reshaped by AI in Different Regions

Commerce, a domain as old as civilization itself, is being redefined in the age of AI. In the West, e-commerce giants like Amazon employ sophisticated AI algorithms to optimize supply chains, predict consumer behavior, and personalize shopping experiences.

On the other hand, in Southeast Asia, platforms like Lazada and Shopee are leveraging AI not just for commerce but also for financial inclusion, offering credit solutions based on AI-driven risk assessments.

In regions like the Middle East, AI is being used to revolutionize the retail experience, with virtual fitting rooms and AI-driven customer service bots. Meanwhile, in Latin America, AI-driven agritech solutions are transforming commerce by optimizing agricultural exports, a significant part of many countries' economies in the region.

While the applications of AI in education and commerce provide a glimpse into the technology's potential for positive transformation, it's also essential to recognize its more controversial uses. One such application, which has garnered global attention, is China's ambitious and somewhat Orwellian Social Credit System. Let's delve deeper into this system and understand its implications for surveillance, society, and the role of AI.

Case Study: China's Social Credit System – Surveillance, Society, and AI

In the vast landscape of AI applications, few systems have garnered as much international attention and scrutiny as China's Social Credit System (SCS). Envisioned as a comprehensive measure to assess and influence the behavior of individuals, companies, and other entities, the SCS is a testament to the power of AI when harnessed for societal monitoring.

At its core, the Social Credit System is designed to aggregate data from various sources, ranging from financial transactions and legal records to social media activity. AI plays a pivotal role in analyzing this vast amount of data, assigning scores based on behaviors deemed desirable or undesirable by the state.

For instance, behaviors like timely payment of bills, charitable donations, or even positive social media posts about the government can lead to higher scores.

Conversely, violations like traffic offenses, spreading misinformation online, or defaulting on loans can result in a reduced score.

The implications of one's social credit score are far-reaching. High scores can lead to benefits such as easier access to loans, priority in job applications, and even discounts on energy bills. On the other hand, a low score can lead to restrictions, like being barred from purchasing flight or train tickets, exclusion from certain high-status jobs, or even public shaming.

While the system is touted by the Chinese government as a means to foster trust and social cohesion, it has raised significant concerns on the global stage. The primary concern revolves around privacy and the potential misuse of data. The system, in many ways, exemplifies the challenges of balancing the benefits of AI-driven governance with the potential risks to individual freedoms and privacy.

While China's approach to integrating AI into governance has been bold and comprehensive, it stands in stark contrast to the more cautious and privacy-centric approach adopted by Europe. As we shift our focus westward, let's delve into the European healthcare sector, where the interplay between AI-driven innovation and the imperative of privacy protection offers valuable insights.

Case Study: AI in European Healthcare - Balancing Innovation and Privacy

Europe's commitment to both technological advancement and individual rights shines brightly in its healthcare sector. As the continent embraces the transformative potential of AI-driven medical solutions, it simultaneously upholds a strong ethos of data privacy and individual rights.

In countries like Germany and France, medical professionals are increasingly relying on AI-driven platforms for image analysis, streamlining the diagnostic process and enhancing accuracy. Meanwhile, in Sweden, AI algorithms assist doctors in predicting patient pathways, enabling a more tailored approach to care.

However, the integration of AI into healthcare is not without challenges. The primary concern remains data privacy. Given the sensitive nature of medical data, it demands the highest levels of protection. European nations, recognizing this imperative, have implemented robust data protection measures. These measures ensure that medical data used in AI applications is handled with the utmost care and transparency.

Before their data is processed by AI tools, patients are typically informed about the intended use of their information and are given the choice to opt-in. This transparent approach ensures that while the healthcare sector reaps the benefits of AI's capabilities, the rights of patients and the sanctity of their data remain uncompromised.

Moreover, the emphasis on explainable AI ensures that AI-driven decisions in healthcare can be understood by both medical professionals and patients. This commitment to transparency addresses the often-cited "black box" nature of AI, ensuring that AI tools are both effective and understandable.

In essence, Europe's approach to AI in healthcare serves as a model, demonstrating that it's possible to harness the benefits of AI while ensuring the protection of individual rights and data privacy.

Conclusion:

As we conclude our exploration of the ethical dimensions of AI, it's evident that the journey is as intricate as it is enlightening. The transformative power of AI, while offering unprecedented benefits, also brings forth a myriad of ethical challenges that societies globally grapple with.

From the personal realms of our relationships to the broader strokes of global governance, AI's influence is pervasive. It's reshaping the very fabric of our societies, redefining norms, and challenging established ethical boundaries. The case studies, from the Cambridge Analytica scandal to the nuanced applications in European healthcare, underscore the real-world implications of these ethical dilemmas.

Yet, amidst these challenges lies the promise of a future where AI and humanity coexist harmoniously. A future where technological advancements don't come at the expense of individual rights or societal values. As we move forward, the onus is on policymakers, technologists, and society at large to collaboratively chart a path that ensures AI's potential is harnessed ethically and responsibly.

The journey of understanding AI's broader impacts on society is a testament to humanity's enduring spirit of innovation and our collective pursuit of a balanced and ethical future.

Chapter 7: AI and the Environment

In the face of escalating environmental challenges, from the pressing threat of climate change to the urgent need for sustainable energy solutions, the world is in dire need of innovative approaches. Enter Artificial Intelligence, a technological marvel that promises not just to revolutionize industries, but also to offer groundbreaking solutions to our planet's most pressing environmental issues. This chapter delves deep into the symbiotic relationship between AI and environmental science, exploring how machine learning, data analytics, and other AI-driven tools are being harnessed to predict, understand, and combat environmental challenges.

The Role of AI in Climate Modeling and Prediction

Climate change, arguably the most significant challenge of our time, demands precise modeling and prediction to understand its trajectory and devise mitigation strategies. Traditional climate models, while robust, often struggle with the vast complexity and sheer volume of data involved. This is where AI steps in, offering a new paradigm in climate science. By harnessing the computational prowess of AI, we can delve deeper, analyze faster, and predict more accurately than ever before. Let's explore the multifaceted ways in which AI is enhancing our understanding of the climate.

1. **Enhanced Data Processing:** With the advent of satellite technology and oceanic sensors, we're inundated with environmental data. AI algorithms, particularly deep learning models, excel at processing this massive influx of data, identifying patterns and anomalies that might be missed by traditional methods.

2. **Predictive Accuracy:** Neural networks, a subset of AI, have shown promise in improving the accuracy of short-term weather predictions. By analyzing vast datasets from various sources, these networks can predict localized weather patterns, severe storm events, and even long-term climatic shifts with increased precision.

3. **Modeling Complex Systems:** The Earth's climate is a complex interplay of atmospheric, terrestrial, and marine systems. AI can model these intricate interactions, providing insights into phenomena like El Niño, polar vortex disruptions, and more.

4. **Real-time Monitoring:** AI-driven tools, combined with satellite imagery, offer real-time monitoring capabilities. This is crucial for tracking rapid environmental changes, such as glacial melts or deforestation events, allowing for timely interventions.

5. **Feedback Loop Integration:** One of the challenges in climate modeling is integrating feedback loops, such as the melting of polar ice reducing the Earth's albedo, leading to more heat

absorption. AI models can dynamically integrate these feedback mechanisms, offering a more holistic view of potential climate trajectories.

The potential of AI in climate science is vast, but it's not without challenges. The accuracy of AI models is contingent on the quality of data they're trained on. Biased or incomplete data can lead to skewed predictions. Moreover, while AI can process and predict, the onus of action still lies with policymakers, businesses, and individuals. AI provides the tools, but it's up to humanity to wield them effectively. And while understanding and predicting our climate's trajectory is vital, equally crucial is the proactive harnessing of AI to develop sustainable solutions for our planet. This leads us to explore how AI is not just a tool for understanding but also for action, especially in the realm of energy and conservation.

AI-driven Solutions for Sustainable Energy and Conservation

The global energy landscape is undergoing a seismic shift. As the world grapples with the dual challenges of increasing energy demand and the urgent need to reduce carbon emissions, the focus has turned to sustainable energy sources and conservation methods. Artificial Intelligence, with its unparalleled data processing and analytical capabilities, is at the forefront of this transformation. As we harness the power of AI, we uncover innovative pathways to not only generate energy more sustainably but also to use it more efficiently. Let's delve into the myriad ways AI is reshaping our approach to energy and conservation.

Optimizing Renewable Energy Sources: One of the challenges with renewable energy, particularly solar and wind, is their variability. AI algorithms can predict energy output based on weather forecasts, optimizing energy storage and distribution. For instance, predicting cloud cover can help in adjusting solar panel angles or storing energy in anticipation of reduced output.

Energy Consumption Analysis: AI-driven systems in homes and industries can analyze energy consumption patterns, providing insights and recommendations to reduce wastage. Smart thermostats, for example, learn from user preferences and adjust heating or cooling for optimal energy use.

Grid Management and Distribution: As energy grids become more complex with the integration of various renewable sources, AI can assist in real-time grid management, ensuring efficient energy distribution and reducing outages.

Predictive Maintenance: Wind turbines, solar panels, and other renewable energy infrastructure benefit from AI-driven predictive maintenance. By analyzing data from sensors, AI can predict when a component might fail, allowing for timely replacements or repairs, thus ensuring uninterrupted energy production.

Conservation through Behavioral Change: AI-driven apps and tools can provide individuals with insights into their energy consumption, nudging them towards more sustainable behaviors. For instance, an app might suggest optimal times to run heavy appliances when renewable energy supply is high.

Natural Resource Management: Beyond energy, AI plays a role in conserving other natural resources. For water conservation, AI can predict usage patterns, detect leaks, and optimize irrigation in agriculture.

The potential of AI in driving sustainable energy solutions and conservation is vast. However, the integration of AI in this sector is not without challenges. Data accuracy, infrastructure costs, and the need for skilled professionals are some of the hurdles to be addressed. Yet, the benefits far outweigh the challenges. As AI continues to evolve, its role in ensuring a sustainable future becomes even more pronounced.

As we reflect on the transformative power of AI in sustainable energy and conservation, it's worth delving deeper into a specific application of AI in this realm.

Let's turn our attention to how AI is revolutionizing renewable energy management.

Case Study: DeepMind's AI in Renewable Energy Management

Google's DeepMind, renowned for its cutting-edge AI research, has ventured into the renewable energy sector, showcasing the transformative potential of AI. Their work with wind energy, in particular, has demonstrated how AI can optimize the generation and distribution of renewable energy.

The Challenge

Wind energy, while sustainable, is notoriously unpredictable. Traditional energy grids, designed for the predictability of fossil fuels, struggle to manage the variability of wind energy. This unpredictability can lead to energy wastage when production exceeds demand and potential blackouts when it falls short.

DeepMind tackled this challenge head-on, developing an AI system that predicts wind energy output 36 hours in advance. Here's how they achieved this:

Predictive Analysis: DeepMind's AI system uses a combination of weather forecasts and historical turbine data to predict wind farm energy output. This allows energy grids to schedule the delivery of wind energy in advance, ensuring it's used more efficiently.

Real-time Adjustments: While the primary focus is on predictive analysis, the system is also designed to make real-time adjustments based on immediate data, ensuring optimal energy distribution at all times.

Enhanced Energy Value: By predicting wind energy production in advance, DeepMind's system has increased the value of wind energy, making it more competitive with traditional energy sources.

The Impact

DeepMind's foray into renewable energy management has yielded impressive results:

- A 20% increase in the value of wind energy.
- Enhanced predictability of wind energy output.
- A significant step towards making renewable energy more viable and mainstream.

In summary, DeepMind's work in the renewable energy sector exemplifies the real-world impact of AI. It's not just about technological advancements; it's about creating tangible solutions to global challenges. As AI continues to evolve, its role in shaping a sustainable future becomes increasingly evident.

Conclusion

As we conclude this exploration into AI's role in environmental solutions, it's evident that the fusion of technology and sustainability is not just a futuristic ideal but a present-day reality. From predicting intricate climate models to optimizing renewable energy sources, AI is playing a pivotal role in addressing some of the most pressing environmental challenges of our time.

DeepMind's endeavors in the renewable energy sector, as highlighted in our case study, serve as a testament to the transformative potential of AI. It's not just about increasing efficiency or reducing costs; it's about creating a sustainable future for generations to come.

However, as with all technological advancements, the journey is ongoing. The challenges are many, and the path is fraught with complexities. But with the combined efforts of researchers, environmentalists, and policymakers, AI offers a beacon of hope. It's a tool that, when wielded with care and foresight, can help us build a more sustainable, eco-friendly world.

As we move forward, it's crucial to continue these discussions, research, and innovations. The symbiotic relationship between AI and the environment is still in its nascent stages, and the possibilities are vast. The onus is on us to harness this potential responsibly, ensuring that as we progress technologically, we also progress sustainably.

Chapter 8: The Future of Transportation: AI on the Move

Transportation, in its essence, has always been a cornerstone of human civilization. From the invention of the wheel to the development of high-speed trains and commercial aircraft, our ability to move from one place to another has been a driving force behind societal progress. Yet, as we stand in the 21st century, the transportation sector finds itself at a crossroads. Urban congestion, environmental concerns, and the sheer demand for more efficient modes of transport have highlighted the need for a significant overhaul.

Enter Artificial Intelligence (AI). This transformative technology, which has already made significant inroads in sectors like healthcare, finance, and entertainment, is now set to redefine the very way we travel. Whether it's the car you drive, the plane you fly in, or the delivery drone that brings your packages, AI is weaving its magic, making transportation smarter, safer, and more efficient.

Imagine a world where traffic jams are a thing of the past, where your car can predict and avoid accidents, where logistics are so optimized that your packages arrive even faster, and where public transport is so efficient that you never have to wait. This isn't a distant dream but a foreseeable future, thanks to AI.

The potential applications are vast. From self-driving cars that promise to make our roads safer to AI-driven air traffic control that could handle the increasing number of flights without a hitch, the possibilities seem endless. And it's not just about making our current modes of transport more efficient. AI also holds the promise of birthing entirely new modes of transportation, ones we haven't even imagined yet.

As we delve deeper into this chapter, we'll explore the myriad ways AI is set to revolutionize transportation. From the algorithms that power autonomous vehicles to the AI-driven innovations in aviation and maritime industries, we're about to embark on a fascinating journey.

And where better to start this journey than with one of the most talked-about innovations of our time: autonomous vehicles. Let's hit the road and explore the future of self-driving cars.

Autonomous Vehicles: The Road Ahead

The Technology Behind Self-Driving Cars: Sensors, Algorithms, and Decision-Making Processes

The dream of a car that can drive itself, once confined to the realms of science fiction, is rapidly becoming a reality. But what makes this possible? At the heart of every autonomous vehicle lies a complex web of technologies that work in tandem to make decisions that were once the sole domain of human drivers. Let's delve into the intricacies of these systems.

Sensors: The Eyes and Ears of the Vehicle

Before a car can make any decision, it first needs to understand its surroundings. This is where sensors come into play. These are the "eyes and ears" of the vehicle, constantly scanning the environment to gather data.

1. **LIDAR (Light Detection and Ranging):** This technology uses lasers to create a 3D map of the surroundings. It can detect objects, their distance, and even their speed, making it invaluable for navigation and obstacle detection.

2. **Cameras:** Multiple cameras are strategically placed around the vehicle, capturing a 360-degree view. Advanced computer vision algorithms then analyze these images to identify road signs, pedestrians, other vehicles, and more.

3. **Radar:** Especially useful in adverse weather conditions, radar systems can detect large

obstacles and other vehicles, even in fog or heavy rain.

4. **Ultrasonic Sensors:** Typically used for parking, these sensors detect objects in close proximity to the vehicle, helping in maneuvers like parallel parking.

Algorithms: The Brain of the Operation

With data from the sensors streaming in, the next step is processing and interpretation. This is where algorithms, the "brain" of the autonomous vehicle, come into play.

1. **Path Planning:** Once the car knows its environment, it needs to decide the best route. Path planning algorithms evaluate the data and chart out the optimal path, considering factors like traffic, road conditions, and the intended destination.

2. **Object Detection and Classification:** It's not enough to just detect objects; the car needs to know what they are. Is that a pedestrian or a lamppost? A dog or a paper bag blowing across the road? Advanced machine learning models are trained on vast datasets to make these distinctions.

3. **Decision Making:** In a dynamic environment, the car needs to make split-second decisions. Should it brake or swerve? Wait or proceed at a

junction? Decision-making algorithms evaluate the data and the potential outcomes to make the safest choice.

The Decision-Making Process: A Symphony of Systems

All these components work in harmony. For instance, when a pedestrian steps onto the road, the cameras and LIDAR detect them, the object detection algorithm identifies them as a human, and the decision-making algorithm decides to slow down or stop, all in a fraction of a second.

This intricate dance of systems, all working in real-time, is what allows autonomous vehicles to navigate our roads. But it's not just about the technology. As we'll see next, there are significant challenges to overcome, from ensuring safety to navigating the complex world of regulations.

As we transition from the marvel of technology to the real-world implications, it's essential to address the challenges that come with it. Safety, regulations, and public perception are just the tip of the iceberg. Let's delve deeper into these challenges and understand the roadblocks autonomous vehicles face on their journey to mainstream adoption.

The Challenges: Safety Concerns, Regulatory Hurdles, and Public Acceptance

Safety Concerns

The paramount concern with autonomous vehicles is, undoubtedly, safety. While the promise of self-driving cars is to reduce human error – a leading cause of accidents – the technology itself must be foolproof. To understand the depth of these safety challenges, let's delve into the specific issues that developers and regulators are grappling with:

1. **Sensor Reliability:** As advanced as sensors are, they're not immune to errors. Dust, fog, or even a bird's dropping can obscure a camera's view. LIDAR and radar can sometimes be confused by complex environments, leading to misinterpretations.

2. **Software Glitches:** Like any software, the algorithms driving these vehicles can have bugs. A minor glitch could lead to major consequences on the road.

3. **Decision-making Dilemmas:** There are situations where a crash is inevitable. How the car's algorithm chooses to act in such scenarios, often termed as the "trolley problem" in AI ethics, is a significant concern.

Regulatory Hurdles

The legal landscape for autonomous vehicles is still in its infancy, and it varies wildly from one jurisdiction to another. To better grasp the regulatory complexities, let's break down some of the most pressing legal challenges faced by the industry:

1. **Liability Issues:** In the event of a crash, who is responsible? The car's owner, the manufacturer, or the software developer? This is a question that legal systems around the world are grappling with.

2. **Testing and Certification:** What tests should an autonomous vehicle pass before it's deemed roadworthy? Standardizing these tests and ensuring they're rigorous enough is a challenge.

3. **Data Privacy:** These vehicles collect vast amounts of data. Who owns this data? How is it used? Regulatory bodies need to address these questions to protect individual privacy.

Public Acceptance

Even if the technology is perfect and the regulations are in place, the success of autonomous vehicles hinges on public perception. To shed light on this, let's explore the key factors that influence how the public views and interacts with these advanced vehicles:

Trust in Technology: Many people are skeptical about entrusting their lives to a machine. Building this trust is crucial for widespread adoption.

Job Displacement Concerns: There's fear that autonomous vehicles will lead to job losses, especially among drivers. Addressing these economic concerns is vital.

Cultural Shifts: Cars are more than just transportation in many cultures; they're symbols of freedom, status, and even rites of passage. The shift to autonomous vehicles might face resistance on these grounds.

As we navigate these challenges, it's essential to look at real-world implementations of this technology. Companies like Tesla and Waymo aren't just making headlines; they're pioneering the future of transportation.

With these challenges laid out, it's enlightening to delve into the real-world applications and advancements spearheaded by industry giants. Their endeavors not only showcase the potential of autonomous vehicles but also highlight the practical challenges and solutions in this evolving landscape.

Real-world examples: Tesla's Autopilot, Waymo's self-driving taxis

In the realm of autonomous vehicles, few names stand out as prominently as Tesla and Waymo. Their advancements in this field serve as benchmarks for what's possible and provide insights into the future of transportation.

Tesla's Autopilot: Tesla, under the visionary leadership of Elon Musk, has been at the forefront of integrating AI into personal vehicles. Their Autopilot system, while not fully autonomous, offers a suite of advanced driver-assistance features. Using a combination of cameras, ultrasonic sensors, and radar, Tesla vehicles can navigate highways, change lanes, and even park themselves. The company's iterative software updates continually enhance these features, bringing them closer to full autonomy. However, it's essential to note that despite its name, Autopilot still requires driver supervision and intervention.

Waymo's self-driving taxis: A subsidiary of Alphabet Inc. (Google's parent company), Waymo has taken a different approach. Instead of integrating AI into consumer vehicles, they've focused on creating a fleet of fully autonomous taxis. In select cities, users can hail a Waymo taxi that operates without a human driver behind the wheel. These vehicles use a combination of LIDAR, radar, and high-resolution cameras to navigate urban environments safely. Waymo's approach underscores the potential for AI to revolutionize public transportation and ride-sharing services.

As we marvel at these innovations in personal vehicles and taxis, it's crucial to recognize that AI's influence isn't limited to these sectors alone. The broader realm of public transportation is also undergoing a transformation, driven by the same technological forces.

Now, let's delve into how AI is reshaping public transportation and making it more efficient, accessible, and sustainable.

AI in Public Transportation

The realm of public transportation, often seen as the backbone of urban mobility, is undergoing a significant transformation, thanks to the integration of AI. From buses to trains, AI technologies are being harnessed to enhance efficiency, reduce costs, and improve passenger experiences. As we delve deeper into this transformation, it becomes evident how AI is reshaping the very fundamentals of how we commute.

Optimizing Bus and Train Routes: One of the most immediate impacts of AI in public transportation is in route optimization. Traditional bus and train routes, often designed based on historical data and manual assessments, can sometimes be inefficient, leading to delays and overcrowded vehicles. AI algorithms analyze vast amounts of real-time data, from traffic conditions to passenger counts, to dynamically adjust routes. This not only ensures timely arrivals and departures but also helps in evenly distributing passenger loads, reducing the chances of overcrowded or underutilized vehicles.

Predictive Maintenance: The reliability of public transport vehicles is paramount. Breakdowns can lead to significant delays, affecting thousands of passengers. Enter AI-driven predictive maintenance. Instead of following a set maintenance schedule, AI algorithms analyze data from sensors placed on vehicles to predict when parts might fail or when maintenance is needed. This proactive approach ensures that issues are addressed before they become major problems, reducing downtime and maintenance costs. While predictive maintenance is a global trend, certain regions are taking the integration of AI in public transportation to even greater heights. One standout example is Japan, with its innovative use of AI in its renowned train system.

Japan, known for its punctual and efficient train system, has been a pioneer in integrating AI into its railways. One notable example is their use of AI for optimal train scheduling. By analyzing factors like passenger flow, weather conditions, and potential disruptions, AI systems dynamically adjust train schedules to ensure maximum efficiency. For instance, during peak hours or events, the system might increase the frequency of trains, while during off-peak times, it might reduce it to save on operational costs. This dynamic scheduling ensures that passengers always have timely and efficient transport options.

The advancements in public transportation, as impressive as they are, represent just a fraction of AI's potential in the broader transportation sector. As we journey from land to air and sea, AI's influence becomes even more pronounced.

Now, let's soar into the skies and dive into the oceans to explore how AI is revolutionizing the aviation and maritime industries.

AI in Aviation and Maritime Industries

The skies and seas have always been the frontier of human exploration and transportation. Today, with the advent of AI, these domains are undergoing transformative changes, promising safer, more efficient, and environmentally friendly operations.

AI for Flight Optimization: The aviation industry is a significant contributor to global carbon emissions. However, with the integration of AI, airlines are now finding ways to reduce their carbon footprint. Advanced algorithms analyze vast amounts of data to optimize flight paths, ensuring that aircraft use the most efficient routes. This not only reduces flight times but also minimizes fuel consumption. Additionally, predictive maintenance powered by AI can forecast when parts of an aircraft will fail or need replacement. This proactive approach ensures safety and reduces unscheduled maintenance, which can be costly and cause delays.

Autonomous Drones: Beyond the large commercial aircraft, the skies are increasingly being populated by drones. These aren't just the small quadcopters used by hobbyists or photographers. Large autonomous drones are being developed for cargo delivery, capable of carrying significant payloads over long distances. These drones can deliver essential supplies to remote areas, conduct surveillance in sensitive regions, or even assist in disaster relief operations, all while being guided by sophisticated AI systems that ensure they reach their destinations safely.

AI's Role in the Maritime Industry: The vastness of the world's oceans presents a unique set of challenges. AI is stepping in to revolutionize the maritime industry. Imagine large cargo ships crossing oceans without a crew on board. This isn't science fiction; companies are actively developing autonomous ships. These vessels use a combination of sensors, satellite data, and AI algorithms to navigate the seas, avoid obstacles, and ensure cargo reaches its destination safely. Just as in aviation, predictive maintenance plays a crucial role in the maritime industry, ensuring ships remain seaworthy and reducing the risk of maritime accidents.

Companies at the forefront of transportation innovation are already integrating AI into their operations. Airbus, for instance, has been testing self-piloted aircraft, pushing the boundaries of what's possible in aviation. On the other hand, Rolls Royce isn't just a luxury car manufacturer; they've shared visions of AI-powered ships, which could redefine maritime transport in the coming decades.

While the advancements in aviation and maritime industries are undeniably impressive, the broader implications of AI in transportation extend beyond just technological marvels. The integration of AI in our transportation systems has profound environmental and societal ramifications. Let's delve into how AI is not only reshaping our modes of transport but also influencing our environment and the very fabric of our societies.

The Environmental and Societal Impacts of AI in Transportation

The transportation sector has long been a significant contributor to global carbon emissions. As cities grow and populations become more mobile, the need for sustainable and efficient transportation becomes even more critical. Enter AI, with its promise to revolutionize transportation in ways that could have profound environmental and societal benefits.

How AI-driven transportation can reduce carbon emissions

One of the most immediate and tangible benefits of AI in transportation is its potential to reduce carbon emissions. Traditional vehicles, especially those running on fossil fuels, are significant contributors to greenhouse gas emissions. AI can play a pivotal role in mitigating this. Here's how.

Optimized Routes: AI algorithms can analyze traffic patterns, weather conditions, and other variables in real-time to suggest the most fuel-efficient routes. This not only saves time but also reduces the amount of fuel consumed, leading to fewer emissions.

Predictive Maintenance: AI can predict when parts of a vehicle are likely to fail or when they need maintenance. By addressing these issues proactively, vehicles can operate at peak efficiency, reducing unnecessary fuel consumption.

Smart Traffic Management: AI-driven traffic lights and management systems can reduce idling times and congestion, leading to smoother traffic flow and, consequently, less fuel wastage.

The integration of AI in transportation doesn't just stop at making vehicles smarter; it has the potential to transform our very cities.

Reduced Need for Parking: As autonomous vehicles become mainstream, the need for parking spaces could diminish. Cars could potentially drop passengers off and then move to areas where parking is less dense or even return home until they are needed again.

Changes in Infrastructure: With fewer cars parked on streets and in parking garages, urban planners might have more freedom to repurpose these spaces. Imagine green parks where once there were concrete parking structures, or pedestrian zones where cars once idled in traffic.

Societal implications

The ripple effects of AI in transportation extend into various facets of society.

Job Shifts: While there's potential for job losses in sectors like taxi services or trucking, new opportunities might arise in areas like AI maintenance, traffic management, and other tech-driven fields.

Changes in Daily Commutes: With AI optimizing routes, the daily grind of commuting could become more bearable. People might be more willing to live further from urban centers, knowing their commute is optimized.

Accessibility: AI-driven vehicles could be a boon for the elderly or those with disabilities, offering them a newfound sense of mobility and independence.

As we delve deeper into the age of AI, it's evident that its influence on transportation is multifaceted. While the technological advancements are exciting, the broader environmental and societal implications are equally significant. The challenge lies in harnessing these advancements responsibly, ensuring a balance between innovation and the greater good.

With these profound changes on the horizon, it's essential to consider the broader picture. How will AI-driven advancements in one sector, like transportation, ripple out and influence other areas of our lives and our world?

Interconnected Impacts: AI's Ripple Effect in Our World

The transformative power of AI in transportation doesn't exist in isolation. Its influence extends, creating ripples that touch various corners of our society, economy, and environment. Here are some examples:

Interplay with Other Industries: The advancements in AI-driven transportation can stimulate growth in other sectors. For instance, the need for advanced sensors could boost the electronics industry. Efficient transportation can also bolster the tourism sector, making travel more accessible and convenient.

Sustainable Development Goals (SDGs): AI in transportation directly aligns with several of the United Nations' SDGs, particularly those related to sustainable cities and communities, affordable and clean energy, and climate action. By reducing emissions and promoting efficient use of resources, AI can play a pivotal role in steering the world towards a more sustainable future.

Sociocultural Shifts: As AI-driven transportation becomes mainstream, it could influence societal norms and values. For instance, the notion of car ownership might change, with more people opting for shared mobility solutions. This shift could also foster a sense of community, as shared transportation modes become the norm.

Global Collaboration: The challenges posed by AI in transportation – be it regulatory hurdles, technological barriers, or ethical dilemmas – are universal. Addressing them offers an opportunity for nations to collaborate, share best practices, and drive global standards.

Innovation Ecosystem: The push for AI in transportation can lead to the sprouting of innovation hubs and research centers dedicated to AI and mobility. This could foster a culture of innovation, attracting talent and investments, and positioning regions or countries as leaders in the AI transportation domain.

Conclusion

As we conclude our exploration of AI in transportation, it's evident that we're not just discussing a technological shift. It's a societal transformation, a reimagining of how we move, interact, and exist in our urban landscapes. The ripples of this transformation extend far beyond the roads, skies, and seas. They touch our industries, our values, our aspirations, and our collective vision for the future.

The journey of understanding AI's role in transportation is akin to peeling layers of an onion. With each layer, new facets, challenges, and opportunities emerge. As we stand on the cusp of this new era, it's imperative for stakeholders – from policymakers to the general public – to engage, deliberate, and shape this journey. For in the balance lies not just the future of transportation, but the blueprint of a sustainable, inclusive, and innovative world.

Chapter 9: AI in Space Exploration and Astronomy

Throughout history, the vast expanse of the cosmos has captivated human imagination. Early civilizations gazed at the stars, seeking patterns and meanings. With the invention of the telescope, our perspective expanded, revealing a universe filled with galaxies, stars, and planets. The 20th century marked a significant leap with the onset of space exploration. From the launch of Sputnik to the Apollo moon landings, humanity showcased its potential to venture beyond our planet.

Now, in the 21st century, we're on the brink of another transformative era in space science, driven by Artificial Intelligence. AI's capabilities—processing vast data, making precise predictions, and adaptive learning— offer tools that can redefine our cosmic endeavors. With AI, we can analyze the enormous data sets from telescopes faster than ever before, predict cosmic events with higher accuracy, and assist astronauts during complex space missions.

AI's role in space isn't just supplementary; it's revolutionary. It can accelerate our pace of discoveries, from spotting distant exoplanets to deciphering the enigmas of dark matter. As we set our sights on ambitious goals like settling on Mars or deep-space exploration, AI stands as an invaluable ally, ready to tackle challenges and enhance mission success rates.

This union of AI and space exploration heralds a promising phase in our journey to understand the universe. It's a collaboration that might provide answers to age-old questions about our place in the cosmos.

With this backdrop, let's dive into the specifics, starting with AI's capability in predicting and understanding cosmic events.

Deep Space Analysis: AI in Cosmic Event Prediction

The universe is a dynamic, ever-evolving entity. From the mesmerizing dance of galaxies to the unpredictable eruptions of stars, cosmic events occur on scales that are both vast and intricate. Predicting these events has always been a challenge, primarily due to the sheer volume of variables involved and the limitations of human-led analysis. However, the advent of AI is transforming this landscape, offering tools that can sift through the cosmic noise to detect patterns and make accurate predictions.

To appreciate the role of AI in this domain, one must first understand the intricacies of predicting cosmic events. The universe doesn't operate on simple, linear principles. It's governed by a set of physical laws that interact in complex ways. For instance, predicting a solar flare isn't just about monitoring a sunspot; it involves understanding magnetic field interactions, plasma physics, and even the history of solar activity. Similarly, tracking an asteroid's path requires data on its composition, the gravitational influences it encounters, and its past trajectory.

Enter AI. With its ability to process vast datasets quickly and its proficiency in pattern recognition, AI is uniquely positioned to assist astronomers. Traditional data analysis might involve manually sifting through telescope images or spectral data, looking for anomalies or patterns. But AI algorithms can automate this process, analyzing data at speeds previously deemed impossible.

For instance, neural networks, a subset of AI, can be trained on existing datasets to recognize specific cosmic phenomena. Once trained, these networks can then scan new data, identifying and predicting events with a high degree of accuracy. This not only speeds up the analysis but also reduces the chances of human oversight.

Real-World Applications: AI in Action

Several groundbreaking projects underscore the potential of AI in cosmic event prediction:

Solar Flares: These dramatic eruptions from the sun's surface can have significant implications for Earth, affecting satellite operations and even power grids. AI models have been developed to predict these flares by analyzing magnetic field data from the sun's surface. Early results have shown that these models can predict flares several hours in advance, with a higher accuracy rate than traditional methods.

Asteroid Tracking: The potential threat of an asteroid impact has led to global efforts to track Near-Earth Objects (NEOs). AI algorithms are now being used to analyze telescope data, identifying moving objects against the backdrop of fixed stars. This allows for quicker identification and tracking of potential hazardous asteroids.

Black Hole Behaviors: Black holes, regions of spacetime exhibiting gravitational acceleration so strong that nothing can escape from it, remain one of the universe's most enigmatic entities. AI is aiding in understanding their behaviors, especially in detecting the gravitational waves they produce when they merge.

The synergy between AI and astronomy is still in its nascent stages. As our algorithms become more sophisticated and our datasets more comprehensive, the potential for breakthroughs in cosmic event prediction grows exponentially. It's a collaboration that promises to expand our understanding of the universe, making the vastness of space a little more comprehensible.

As we marvel at these advancements in deep space analysis, it's equally crucial to explore how AI aids in the broader mapping of the cosmos. Let's delve into the realm of cosmic cartography and see how AI is charting the universe's vast expanse.

Cosmic Cartography: Mapping the Universe with AI

The universe, in its infinite vastness, presents a daunting challenge to those who seek to map it. From the luminous stars that dot the night sky to the dark matter that eludes direct observation, charting the cosmos is an endeavor that pushes the boundaries of human knowledge and capability. Traditional methods, while groundbreaking in their time, often fall short in the face of the sheer magnitude of data the universe offers. This is where Artificial Intelligence, with its unparalleled analytical prowess, steps in, promising a new era in cosmic cartography.

The Challenges of Charting the Vast Expanse

Space is vast, and that's an understatement. The observable universe is estimated to be 93 billion light-years in diameter. Within this expanse lie billions of galaxies, each housing billions of stars, planets, and other celestial bodies. Mapping this requires not only capturing images and data but also interpreting them, understanding anomalies, and predicting patterns. Traditional methods, relying on human observation and manual data analysis, are often overwhelmed by the sheer volume and complexity of the information.

Moreover, many cosmic phenomena are transient or subtle. A distant star's flicker might indicate an orbiting planet, or it might be just noise in the data. Distinguishing between these requires precision and a deep understanding of cosmic processes.

AI: The New Astronomer's Tool

Artificial Intelligence offers tools that can process vast amounts of data quickly, recognize patterns, and even learn from previous datasets to improve future predictions. One of the primary ways AI aids in cosmic cartography is through data analysis from telescopes and satellites. These instruments capture a plethora of information, from visual images to radiation spectra. AI algorithms, especially machine learning models, can sift through this data, identifying patterns, anomalies, or events of interest.

For instance, when telescopes capture images of the night sky, AI can be used to enhance these images, remove noise, and highlight areas of interest. In the realm of spectral data, AI can identify signatures that might indicate the presence of specific elements, temperatures, or radiation sources.

Neural Networks and the Hunt for Exoplanets

One of the most exciting applications of AI in astronomy is the hunt for exoplanets—planets that orbit stars outside our solar system. Identifying these distant worlds is challenging. They don't emit their own light, and their signals are often drowned out by the blinding light of their parent stars.

Neural networks, a type of machine learning model, have proven to be particularly adept at this task. By training on datasets where exoplanets have been confirmed, these networks learn the subtle signals that indicate a planet's presence. Once trained, they can scan new data, identifying potential exoplanets with a high degree of accuracy.

For example, NASA's Kepler mission, which sought to identify Earth-like planets orbiting other stars, employed machine learning to enhance its data analysis. By using a neural network, researchers were able to identify 50 new exoplanets, adding to the mission's already impressive tally.

The collaboration between AI and astronomy is a testament to humanity's enduring quest for knowledge. As we employ more sophisticated AI tools and gather more comprehensive data, our cosmic maps will become more detailed, and our understanding of the universe will deepen.

As we stand on the cusp of these new discoveries, it's essential to recognize that our exploration isn't limited to passive observation. The next frontier involves active exploration, with AI playing a pivotal role in pioneering missions beyond our planet. Let's delve into the realm of AI-driven space missions and the promise they hold for interplanetary exploration.

AI-Driven Space Missions: Pioneering Interplanetary Exploration

The final frontier, as space is often termed, has always been a realm of challenges and mysteries. From the early days of space exploration, when humans first broke free from Earth's gravitational pull, to the present day, with plans for Mars colonization and deep-space probes, the journey has been marked by innovation, determination, and a thirst for knowledge. As we venture further into space, the challenges multiply, but so do our technological capabilities. One of the most transformative technologies shaping the future of space exploration is Artificial Intelligence.

The Evolution of Space Missions and the Integration of AI

Historically, space missions were heavily reliant on ground-based control. Astronauts and space probes followed predetermined paths, with every maneuver planned in advance. While this approach served well for early missions, as we aim for more distant and complex targets, the need for real-time decision-making and autonomy becomes paramount. This is especially true for missions beyond Mars, where communication delays can span from minutes to hours.

Enter AI. With the ability to process vast amounts of data, make decisions based on complex algorithms, and learn from past experiences, AI has become an invaluable tool for modern space missions. It offers the promise of autonomous operations, where spacecraft can make decisions without waiting for instructions from Earth.

AI in Navigation, Communication, and Decision-making

One of the primary roles of AI in space missions is navigation. Space is filled with hazards, from asteroids to space debris. AI-driven sensors and algorithms can detect these hazards in real-time, adjusting the spacecraft's path to avoid collisions. This is particularly crucial for missions that aim to land on other planets or celestial bodies, where the terrain is unknown and filled with potential dangers.

Communication is another area where AI plays a pivotal role. With the vast distances involved in space exploration, traditional communication methods become less effective. AI can optimize communication protocols, ensuring that data is transmitted efficiently and without loss.

Furthermore, AI aids in decision-making. For instance, if a spacecraft encounters an unexpected situation, AI algorithms can analyze the scenario, weigh the potential risks and benefits, and decide on the best course of action, all without human intervention.

Real-world Applications: Pioneering the Cosmos with AI

Several modern space missions have integrated AI to enhance their capabilities. Space probes sent to the far reaches of our solar system, for instance, use AI to autonomously handle operations, from adjusting their course to managing their instruments.

One notable example is satellite swarm coordination. As we deploy more satellites, managing their movements to avoid collisions becomes a complex task. AI algorithms can coordinate the movements of these satellite swarms, ensuring they function as a cohesive unit without interference.

Another application is in the realm of space rovers. These vehicles, sent to explore the surfaces of other planets, are becoming increasingly autonomous. They can navigate challenging terrains, decide which samples to collect, and even conduct basic analyses, all thanks to AI.

Looking to the Red Planet and Beyond

The integration of AI in space missions is not just about enhancing current capabilities; it's about enabling new possibilities. As we set our sights on more distant and challenging targets, from the red sands of Mars to the icy moons of Jupiter, AI will be at the forefront, guiding our way and ensuring our success.

As we reflect on the profound impact of AI on space exploration, it's worth delving deeper into specific missions that have harnessed this technology to its fullest. One such mission, which stands as a testament to the synergy between AI and space exploration, is the Mars Rover mission. Let's explore this fascinating confluence of technology and ambition.

Case Study: AI in the Mars Rover Missions

The Mars Rover missions, spearheaded by NASA, have been monumental in our quest to understand our neighboring planet. These robotic explorers, traversing the Martian landscape, have sent back invaluable data, reshaping our understanding of Mars and its history. But behind their success lies a silent partner, one that has been instrumental in navigating challenges and maximizing the potential of these missions: Artificial Intelligence.

From the early days of the Sojourner rover, part of the Mars Pathfinder mission in the late 1990s, to the more recent Perseverance rover, AI has played an increasingly significant role. Initially, AI's involvement was limited, aiding in basic navigational tasks and data processing. But as the rovers evolved, so did the role of AI.

For instance, the Curiosity rover, which landed on Mars in 2012, was equipped with AI-driven algorithms that allowed it to make decisions autonomously. Instead of waiting for commands from Earth, which could take anywhere from 4 to 24 minutes due to the vast distance, Curiosity could analyze its surroundings, identify potential obstacles, and chart its own course.

Challenges and AI-Driven Solutions

The Martian environment is harsh and unpredictable. Dust storms can reduce visibility, and the rugged terrain is filled with obstacles, from large boulders to deep craters. Navigating this landscape is a challenge, but one that AI has been instrumental in addressing.

Using a combination of cameras and sensors, the rovers can create a 3D map of their surroundings. AI algorithms then process this data, identifying potential hazards and plotting a safe path. This not only ensures the rover's safety but also allows it to reach areas of scientific interest more efficiently.

Data collection is another area where AI has proven invaluable. The rovers are equipped with a suite of scientific instruments, from spectrometers to cameras. AI algorithms can analyze the data in real-time, identifying points of interest. For instance, if a rover's spectrometer detects a mineral of interest, AI can prompt the rover to investigate further, taking additional samples or photographs.

The success of the AI-driven Mars Rover missions has set a precedent for future space exploration. The ability to operate autonomously, make real-time decisions, and process vast amounts of data on-the-fly has proven invaluable. As we set our sights on more distant targets, from the icy moons of Jupiter and Saturn to potential exoplanets, the role of AI will only grow.

The lessons learned from the Mars Rover missions will be instrumental in shaping these future missions. The challenges will be greater, the distances vaster, but with AI by our side, the potential for discovery is limitless.

In the vast expanse of space, with its myriad mysteries and challenges, AI stands as a beacon, guiding our way. As we reflect on the achievements of the Mars Rover missions and look to the future, one thing is clear: AI will be at the forefront, helping us unravel the cosmic mysteries that await. Let's delve deeper into what the future might hold for AI in space exploration.

The Future Horizon: AI's Potential in Unraveling Cosmic Mysteries

As we stand on the precipice of a new era in space exploration, the potential roles of Artificial Intelligence stretch as vast and infinite as the cosmos itself. The achievements of AI in current space missions, as showcased by the Mars Rovers, are just the tip of the iceberg. The future beckons with promises of deeper space exploration, understanding of cosmic phenomena, and even the potential colonization of other planets.

The next generation of space missions will undoubtedly be more complex, aiming to reach farther and explore deeper. AI will play a pivotal role in these missions, from navigating through asteroid belts to analyzing the atmospheres of distant exoplanets for signs of life. Advanced AI algorithms might be used to simulate space missions, predicting potential challenges and outcomes before a mission is even launched. This kind of predictive modeling could save time, resources, and even lives.

The dream of colonizing another planet, once the stuff of science fiction, is slowly becoming a tangible goal. Whether you see this as good or bad, AI will be instrumental in this endeavor. From selecting the ideal planet or moon based on vast datasets to building sustainable habitats in alien environments, AI's role will be multifaceted.

Imagine AI-driven robots constructing habitats on Mars or the Moon, preparing for human arrival. These robots could use resources available on these celestial bodies, reducing the need to transport materials from Earth. Once humans arrive, AI systems could assist in daily operations, from optimizing energy consumption to predicting potential weather anomalies.

Ethical and Logistical Considerations

However, with great potential comes great responsibility. The integration of AI in space missions brings forth a plethora of ethical and logistical considerations. For instance, should an AI-driven spacecraft make decisions that prioritize the mission's success over the safety of astronauts on board? How do we ensure that AI systems, when operating autonomously in space, adhere to international space treaties and laws?

Logistically, the challenges are immense. Ensuring seamless communication between AI systems in deep space and control centers on Earth, especially when there's a significant time lag, will be crucial. Moreover, these AI systems need to be robust, capable of self-repair, given the difficulty of sending repair missions to distant locations.

Conclusion

The fusion of AI and space exploration is a testament to human ingenuity and our relentless quest for knowledge. As we venture into the unknown, AI stands as our ally, illuminating the path and ensuring our journey is efficient, safe, and filled with discoveries. The challenges are monumental, but the potential rewards –

understanding our universe better and possibly finding a new home among the stars – make the journey worth every risk. As we close this chapter, we're reminded that the horizon of possibilities with AI is as boundless as space itself, and our exploration of both is just beginning.

Chapter 10: The Intersection of AI and Art

Art, in its myriad forms, has always been a reflection of humanity's soul, capturing our emotions, aspirations, and the essence of our existence. From the earliest cave paintings to contemporary digital art, every piece tells a story of its era, its creators, and the society that shaped it. Now, as we stand at the crossroads of technology and creativity, a new artist emerges from the binary world of zeros and ones: Artificial Intelligence. This chapter delves into the fascinating realm where AI meets art, exploring the capabilities, the controversies, and the profound implications of this union.

AI in Music Composition, Visual Arts, and Literature

The world of art is vast and varied, encompassing a plethora of mediums and genres. With the advent of AI, each of these domains is experiencing a transformative shift, challenging traditional paradigms and birthing new possibilities.

Music Composition: The realm of music has always been a playground for innovation. Today, AI-driven algorithms are composing symphonies, creating unique soundscapes, and even improvising alongside human musicians. Tools like OpenAI's MuseNet can generate compositions in a variety of styles, from classical to contemporary. These AI compositions, while technically sound, spark debates about the soul and emotion behind the notes.

Visual Arts: In the visual arts, AI is not just a tool but also a collaborator. Artists are using AI algorithms to create intricate patterns, reimagine classic artworks, and even produce original pieces. Deep learning models, trained on thousands of artworks, can now generate paintings that are auctioned alongside human-created art. These creations, while visually stunning, raise questions about originality and the essence of creativity.

Literature: The literary world isn't untouched by AI's influence. Algorithms are now writing poetry, short stories, and even attempting novels. While the syntax and structure might be impeccable, the depth of emotion and the nuances of human experience are areas of contention. Can an AI truly capture the human condition in its prose, or is it merely mimicking patterns it has learned?

The integration of AI in these artistic domains is undeniably impressive, showcasing the vast potential of machine learning and deep learning models. However, it also brings forth a plethora of questions. Is AI truly 'creating' or merely 'generating' based on patterns? Can a machine understand the depth of human emotion that often drives art? Does the introduction of AI in art diminish the value of human-created pieces?

These questions lead us to a broader, more philosophical debate, one that delves into the very essence of creativity and computation.

The Debate: Creativity vs. Computation

Art, in its purest form, is often seen as an expression of human emotion, experience, and imagination. It's a realm where creativity reigns supreme, where the intangible feelings are given form, and where the soul speaks louder than logic. Enter Artificial Intelligence, a product of human ingenuity, grounded in logic, algorithms, and computation. As AI begins to produce art, a fundamental question arises: Can true creativity be computed?

At the heart of this debate lies the understanding of what creativity truly is. Historically, creativity has been viewed as a uniquely human trait, an amalgamation of our experiences, emotions, and innate talent. It's spontaneous, unpredictable, and often defies logic. Artists often speak of inspiration coming from a muse, a moment, or even a memory. This intangible spark is what leads to masterpieces that resonate across generations.

AI, on the other hand, operates in the realm of logic. It learns from data, identifies patterns, and generates outputs based on algorithms. When AI creates art, it's essentially drawing from vast datasets of existing art, finding patterns, and producing something that fits within those recognized patterns. While the results can be technically perfect and even beautiful, critics argue that it lacks the soul and originality of human-created art.

However, it's essential to recognize that the line between creativity and computation isn't black and white. Many artists use logical methods, structures, and even algorithms in their creative process. Music has scales and rhythms, painting has techniques and principles, and literature has grammar and structure. So, is it entirely implausible to think that an AI, given the right algorithms, can't tap into a form of creativity?

AI as a Tool vs. AI as an Artist: Another perspective in this debate is viewing AI as a tool rather than an independent artist. Just as a painter uses a brush or a musician uses an instrument, artists can use AI to enhance, augment, or even challenge their creative processes. In this light, AI becomes a collaborator, bringing its computational strength to the table, while the human artist infuses emotion, meaning, and depth.

The Audience's Role: Art is not just about the creator but also the beholder. An AI-generated piece of music or painting that evokes emotion, thought, or any reaction from its audience surely holds value. If art's purpose is to make one feel, think, or reflect, does it matter if the source is human or machine?

As we delve deeper into this era of AI-generated art, these questions will continue to challenge artists, critics, and audiences alike. The intersection of creativity and computation is a new frontier, one that holds immense potential and equally significant philosophical dilemmas.

As we ponder on this debate, it's intriguing to delve into real-world applications where AI has not just mimicked but also innovated in the realm of art. One such fascinating foray is in the world of music, where AI has ventured into the intricate and soulful domain of jazz improvisation.

Case Study: "DeepJazz: AI's Foray into Jazz Improvisation"

Jazz, with its intricate melodies, spontaneous improvisations, and soulful rhythms, has always been seen as a pinnacle of human creativity in music. It's a genre where the artist communicates not just with the audience but also with fellow musicians in real-time, creating a dynamic, ever-evolving soundscape. So, when AI steps into this realm, it's not just a technological feat but also a philosophical challenge.

Enter "DeepJazz," an AI-driven project that sought to capture the essence of jazz improvisation.

DeepJazz was born out of a passion project by a computer scientist and jazz enthusiast. The goal was simple yet ambitious: to create an AI model that could understand the nuances of jazz and produce its own improvisations. Using deep learning, a subset of machine learning that mimics the neural networks of the human brain, the project aimed to teach a machine the art of jazz.

The first step was feeding the AI a vast amount of jazz music, from classics by Miles Davis and John Coltrane to contemporary pieces. The AI, over time, began to recognize patterns, structures, and even the subtle nuances that make jazz, jazz. It learned the scales, the chord progressions, and the unpredictable nature of improvisations.

Once trained, DeepJazz was tasked with creating its own pieces. And the results were astonishing. The AI-produced music had the technical aspects of jazz down to a tee. The improvisations, while not as spontaneous as a human's, had a rhythm and flow that were unmistakably jazz. However, some critics argued that while the music was technically sound, it lacked the "soul" or "feel" of human-produced jazz.

DeepJazz was not without its critics. Purists argued that jazz is an expression of human experience, emotion, and spontaneity, something a machine can never truly replicate. Others felt that while the project was technologically impressive, it didn't capture the essence of jazz. There were also concerns about what such advancements meant for human musicians. Would AI replace them? Or would it be used as a tool to aid human creativity?

DeepJazz opened the door to a new realm of possibilities. Following its success, several other projects emerged, exploring AI's potential in different music genres. While the debate about creativity vs. computation rages on, one thing is clear: AI has a role to play in the future of music, whether as a collaborator, a tool, or even as an independent artist.

Conclusion

The intersection of AI and art is a testament to the limitless possibilities of human innovation. As we've journeyed through this chapter, from the realms of music composition to visual arts and literature, and delved into the debates surrounding creativity and computation, it's evident that AI's role in art is both transformative and controversial.

Art, at its core, is an expression of the human experience. And while AI can replicate patterns, techniques, and even styles, the soul of art lies in its imperfections, its emotions, and its ability to resonate with the human spirit. AI, in its current form, serves as a tool, a collaborator, enhancing and challenging the artistic process.

As we look to the future, the convergence of AI and art will continue to spark debates, inspire innovations, and challenge our perceptions of creativity. The canvas is vast, and the brushstrokes of AI are just beginning to shape it. The next chapters of this symbiotic relationship between man, machine, and art are yet to be written, and they promise to be as intriguing as they are unpredictable.

Chapter 11: AI in Sports and Fitness

From the ancient Olympic Games in Greece to the high-tech stadiums of today, sports have always been a reflection of the times. They not only showcase human physical prowess but also the technological advancements of an era. In the early 20th century, the introduction of slow-motion replays transformed how we viewed critical moments in a game. Later, computer simulations and video analysis tools provided coaches with insights that were previously unimaginable. Today, we stand at the cusp of another transformative era in sports, driven by Artificial Intelligence.

The journey of technology in sports has been nothing short of remarkable. In the 1960s, the advent of televised sports brought games to living rooms, bridging distances and creating global fans. The late 20th century saw the rise of computer simulations, allowing teams to analyze plays and devise strategies. Wearable tech, like heart rate monitors, gave athletes real-time data on their performance. But these were just the precursors to a more profound change.

With the 21st century came the explosion of data. Sensors became more advanced, capturing every minute detail – from an athlete's stride length to their hydration levels. This deluge of data, while valuable, posed a new challenge: How to process and make sense of it all?

Enter Artificial Intelligence. AI, with its ability to process vast amounts of data and identify patterns, has become an invaluable tool in the sports industry. It's not just about number crunching; AI systems can predict player injuries, suggest optimal training regimens, and even help in talent scouting. In fitness, AI-driven apps provide personalized workout and diet plans, adapting in real-time based on user feedback.

But it's not just the athletes and coaches who benefit. Fans, too, are experiencing sports in a way they never have before. AI-driven virtual reality experiences, predictive game analyses, and personalized content delivery are enhancing the fan experience, making them feel more connected to the game and their favorite players.

As we delve deeper into this chapter, we'll explore the multifaceted ways AI is impacting sports and fitness, from team strategies to personal training regimes. The playing field is evolving, and AI is at the heart of this transformation.

With this backdrop, let's first dive into one of the most significant areas of impact: team sports. How are coaches, strategists, and players harnessing the power of AI to gain a competitive edge? The world of predictive analytics in team sports awaits our exploration.

Predictive Analytics in Team Sports Strategy

The Rise of Data-Driven Decision-Making in Sports

In the realm of sports, intuition, talent, and experience have traditionally been the guiding lights for players and coaches alike. The roar of the crowd, the gut feeling of a coach, and the instincts of a player often dictated the flow and outcome of a game. However, the 21st century ushered in a new player onto the field, one that doesn't wear a jersey or lace up boots but has an undeniable influence on the game: data.

The inception of data-driven decision-making in sports can be traced back to the late 20th century, but it was the 2000s that truly marked its ascendancy. The Moneyball era of baseball, popularized by Michael Lewis's book and the subsequent film, highlighted how the Oakland Athletics used statistical analysis to assemble a competitive team despite a limited budget. This approach challenged traditional scouting methods, emphasizing the importance of on-base percentage and slugging percentage over often overvalued metrics. The success of the Athletics opened the floodgates for a data revolution in sports.

With advancements in technology, the volume of data available exploded. Wearable sensors, high-speed cameras, and advanced tracking systems began capturing every move of a player, every pass of a ball, and every stride on the field. Suddenly, teams had access to metrics like a player's heart rate, distance covered, speed, and much more. This granular data provided insights that were previously invisible to the naked eye.

But it wasn't just about collecting data; it was about making sense of it. Teams started hiring data analysts and statisticians, creating a bridge between the raw numbers and actionable insights. These professionals began to dissect every aspect of the game, from player positioning and ball movement to opponent strategies. The goal was clear: to gain a competitive edge.

The influence of data-driven decision-making wasn't limited to team selection or player acquisition. It permeated every facet of the game. Coaches began to rely on data to devise game strategies, identify weaknesses in the opposition, and optimize player performance. In-game decisions, like when to substitute a player or which play to execute in a crucial moment, started being informed by real-time data.

This shift towards a more analytical approach was met with skepticism by some traditionalists. They argued that the essence of sports, the unpredictability, and the human element, was being overshadowed by cold, hard numbers. However, the results spoke for themselves.

Teams that embraced this new paradigm started seeing success, forcing others to adapt or be left behind.

Today, data-driven decision-making is not just a trend but a staple in sports. From football and basketball to tennis and cricket, analytics play a pivotal role in shaping the modern game. The blend of traditional sports wisdom with cutting-edge data analysis has created a richer, more nuanced understanding of sports, benefiting players, coaches, and fans alike.

While the rise of data in sports has been transformative, the real magic lies in how this data is processed and interpreted. This is where Artificial Intelligence steps in, turning vast streams of data into actionable insights. Let's delve into how AI is revolutionizing the way we understand and analyze sports data.

How AI Processes and Interprets Vast Amounts of Game Data

The world of sports generates an immense volume of data every second. From the trajectory of a soccer ball to the acceleration of a sprinter, from the spin rate of a tennis serve to the force exerted in a rugby tackle, every action and movement is a potential data point. But raw data, in its unprocessed form, is like an uncut diamond; its true value is realized only when it's refined. This is where Artificial Intelligence (AI) comes into play.

1. Data Collection: Before AI can process data, it needs to be collected. Advanced technologies like motion-capture cameras, wearable sensors, and GPS trackers capture thousands of data points during a game. For instance, in a single football match, data about player movements, ball possession, passes, shots, tackles, and more are recorded.

2. Data Cleaning: Not all data collected is useful. Redundant or irrelevant data can skew analysis. AI algorithms preprocess this data, filtering out noise and ensuring that only pertinent information is considered. This step is crucial to ensure the accuracy of subsequent analyses.

3. Pattern Recognition: One of AI's strengths is its ability to recognize patterns in vast datasets, patterns that might be invisible to the human eye. For example, an AI system can analyze hundreds of hours of game footage to identify a specific team's defensive strategy or a player's preferred moves.

4. Predictive Analysis: AI doesn't just analyze the past; it predicts the future. By processing historical data, AI can make predictions about future events. This could range from forecasting a player's injury risk based on their play style and physical metrics to predicting the outcome of a match based on team performance data.

5. Real-time Analysis: Sports are dynamic, and decisions often need to be made in the blink of an eye. AI can process data in real-time, providing coaches, players, and analysts with instant insights. For instance, during a basketball game, AI can analyze the opposition's play patterns and suggest defensive strategies on the fly.

6. Visualization: Data, especially in large volumes, can be challenging to understand. AI assists in visualizing this data, converting complex patterns and trends into graphs, heat maps, and other visual formats that are easier to interpret. A coach can, for instance, get a heat map of where a soccer player spent most of their time during a match, providing insights into player positioning and movement.

The integration of AI in processing and interpreting sports data is a game-changer. It offers a depth of analysis previously unimaginable. However, it's essential to remember that AI is a tool, not a replacement for human expertise. While it provides valuable insights, the final decisions still rest with the players, coaches, and analysts. They use AI-derived insights to inform their decisions, combining the best of machine intelligence with human intuition and experience.

Having understood the mechanics of how AI processes sports data, it's equally crucial to see this technology in action. Let's explore some real-world applications where AI's analytical prowess is making tangible impacts, from enhancing player performance to predicting injuries and optimizing game strategies.

Real-world Applications: Player Performance Analysis, Injury Prediction, and Game Strategy Optimization

The fusion of AI with sports analytics has ushered in a new era of precision, enabling teams and athletes to gain a competitive edge. Here's a closer look at how AI-driven insights are being applied in real-world scenarios:

Player Performance Analysis:

In the past, player evaluations were primarily based on subjective observations. Today, AI provides an objective lens, analyzing every aspect of a player's game. For instance, in basketball, AI can evaluate a player's shooting technique by analyzing the arc of their shot, release time, and posture. In football, AI can assess a player's passing accuracy, ball control, and positioning. These insights help coaches tailor training programs to individual player needs, enhancing their strengths and addressing their weaknesses.

Injury Prediction:

Injuries are an athlete's worst nightmare. AI is playing a pivotal role in minimizing this risk. By analyzing data from wearable sensors, AI can identify subtle changes in an athlete's movement or biomechanics that might indicate fatigue or strain. For example, a slight alteration in a tennis player's serve motion might suggest shoulder stress. By catching these early signs, interventions can be made before minor issues escalate into major injuries.

Game Strategy Optimization:

AI's ability to process vast amounts of game data means it can identify patterns and trends that might go unnoticed by human analysts. For instance, AI can analyze an opposing team's defensive setup in soccer, identifying weak points that can be exploited. In cricket, AI can assess a bowler's delivery patterns, helping batsmen anticipate the type of ball they're likely to face next.

These applications are just the tip of the iceberg. As AI continues to evolve, its integration into sports analytics will only deepen, offering even more nuanced insights.

While the applications of AI in sports are undeniably transformative, they also bring forth a new set of challenges and considerations, especially for those at the helm of decision-making. How do coaches and team strategists balance AI-derived insights with their instincts? How is the dynamic of coaching altered in an age where algorithms can suggest game strategies? Let's delve into the profound impact of AI on coaching decisions and in-game strategies.

The Impact on Coaching Decisions and In-Game Strategies

The integration of AI into sports has undeniably provided coaches with a treasure trove of data-driven insights. However, with this wealth of information comes the challenge of how to best utilize it without overshadowing the human element intrinsic to sports. Let's delve deeper into the specific ways AI's analytical prowess is influencing coaching decisions and strategies on the field.

Augmented Decision-Making:

Coaches have traditionally relied on their intuition, experience, and observational skills to make decisions. With AI, they now have an additional layer of data-driven recommendations. For instance, during a basketball game, AI might suggest a specific player substitution based on fatigue levels or an opponent's current lineup. While this information is invaluable, the final decision still rests with the coach, who must weigh the AI's suggestion against their understanding of the game's flow and player morale.

Dynamic Strategy Adjustments:

In the past, teams would often stick to a pre-determined game plan. Now, with real-time AI analysis, strategies can be adjusted on the fly. If AI detects that an opposing soccer team is consistently exploiting a particular flank, coaches can make immediate tactical changes to counteract this. This dynamic approach ensures that teams are always one step ahead, but it also demands that coaches be adaptable and open to altering their game plan based on AI insights.

Enhancing Player-Coach Communication:

AI can serve as a bridge between players and coaches. With objective data at their fingertips, coaches can provide specific feedback, helping players understand areas of improvement. This data-driven approach can eliminate potential biases and ensure that feedback is constructive and actionable.

Ethical Considerations:

While AI offers numerous advantages, it also raises ethical questions. Should a player be benched based solely on AI predictions of potential injury? How much should AI influence the selection of players for a crucial match? Coaches must tread carefully, ensuring that AI aids, rather than dictates, their decisions.

Maintaining the Human Touch:

Despite the influx of technology, sports remain a deeply human endeavor, driven by passion, determination, and spirit. Coaches must ensure that while they leverage AI for tactical advantages, they don't lose sight of the human aspects of the game. Building team morale, fostering camaraderie, and understanding player emotions are areas where human intuition cannot be replaced by algorithms.

While the world of team sports undergoes this transformative phase with AI, there's another domain where AI's influence is burgeoning: personal fitness. As individuals around the world become more health-conscious, AI-driven tools are stepping in, offering personalized training regimens, dietary advice, and performance tracking. Let's explore how AI is reshaping the landscape of personal fitness and training.

AI-Driven Personal Fitness and Training Tools

The Transformation of Personal Fitness with Wearable AI Tech

In the age of digital transformation, personal fitness has undergone a significant metamorphosis. Gone are the days when fitness was solely about hitting the gym, lifting weights, or jogging in the park. Today, it's an amalgamation of technology and traditional workouts, with Artificial Intelligence (AI) playing a pivotal role in this evolution.

Wearable technology has become the cornerstone of modern fitness. From tracking steps to monitoring heart rates, these devices provide a plethora of data that was previously inaccessible to the average individual. But it's not just about data collection; it's about data interpretation. This is where AI steps in.

Smartwatches and fitness bands, equipped with AI algorithms, don't just count steps or measure heart rates; they analyze patterns. For instance, they can detect if a person's heart rate is unusually high for the amount of physical activity they're doing, potentially flagging health issues. They can also monitor sleep patterns, ensuring that users are getting the right amount of restful sleep, which is crucial for recovery and overall health.

Furthermore, these wearables can provide real-time feedback. If you're running, they can suggest if you need to speed up or slow down to stay in a desired heart rate zone. If you're lifting weights, they can analyze if your form is correct or if you're at risk of injury. This immediate feedback loop, powered by AI, ensures that individuals are not just working out but working out right.

Another transformative aspect is the integration of AI-driven virtual trainers in these wearables. Instead of a one-size-fits-all workout video, these virtual trainers adapt in real-time. If you're struggling with a particular exercise, the AI can suggest an alternative or modify the workout intensity. It's like having a personal trainer on your wrist, one that learns and adapts to your fitness level and goals.

The social integration of these wearables further enhances the fitness journey. Many AI-driven fitness apps have a community aspect, allowing users to share their progress, participate in challenges, and even compete with friends. This not only adds a fun element to workouts but also fosters a sense of community and motivation.

In essence, AI-driven wearables have democratized personal fitness. They've made top-notch fitness advice, which was once the preserve of elite athletes and wealthy individuals, accessible to everyone. Whether you're a seasoned athlete or someone just starting on their fitness journey, these devices ensure that you have the best tools at your disposal to achieve your health and fitness goals.

As we marvel at the advancements in wearable AI tech and its profound impact on personal fitness, it's essential to recognize that this is just the tip of the iceberg. The realm of AI in fitness extends beyond wearables, diving deep into personalized workout regimens tailored to individual needs, preferences, and goals.

AI's Role in Creating Personalized Workout Regimens

The age-old adage, "One size does not fit all," rings especially true in the realm of fitness. What works for one individual might not necessarily work for another. Factors such as age, body type, fitness goals, and even genetic makeup can influence how one responds to a particular workout. Recognizing this variability, AI has emerged as a game-changer, crafting personalized workout regimens tailored to individual needs.

At the core of this personalization is data. AI systems, when integrated with wearable devices or fitness apps, continuously collect data on an individual's performance, from the number of reps in a strength training session to the pace and heart rate during a run. But more than just collecting data, AI analyzes it, looking for patterns, strengths, weaknesses, and areas of improvement.

For instance, if an individual consistently struggles to complete a particular exercise or often feels fatigued after a specific workout, AI can identify these patterns. It then adjusts the workout regimen, either by suggesting an alternative exercise or by modifying the intensity and duration. This dynamic adjustment ensures that individuals are always working within their optimal range, maximizing gains while minimizing the risk of injury.

Moreover, AI-driven fitness platforms often come with a feedback mechanism. Users can input how they felt after a workout, any pain or discomfort they experienced, and their energy levels. Over time, the AI system learns from this feedback, further refining the workout regimen to align with the user's feedback and performance data.

Another significant advantage of AI-driven personalized workouts is goal setting. Whether it's weight loss, muscle gain, improving cardiovascular health, or training for a marathon, AI can craft a workout plan specifically designed to achieve that goal. It sets milestones, tracks progress, and if the user is falling behind, it tweaks the plan to ensure the goal remains achievable.

Furthermore, AI can integrate cross-training into workout regimens. Recognizing the benefits of a holistic fitness approach, it can suggest yoga or pilates on certain days to complement strength training, ensuring that the body gets a well-rounded workout.

The beauty of AI-driven personalized workout regimens lies in their adaptability. They evolve as the user evolves, ensuring that the workouts remain challenging yet achievable, pushing individuals just enough to see continuous improvement.

As we delve deeper into the myriad ways AI is revolutionizing fitness, it's not just about the workouts. Nutrition plays a pivotal role in achieving fitness goals, and AI is stepping up to ensure that individuals get the right fuel for their bodies, tailoring meal plans based on specific needs and preferences.

Nutrition and Diet: How AI Tailors Meal Plans Based on Individual Needs

Nutrition is a cornerstone of health and fitness. While exercise shapes and strengthens the body, it's the food we consume that fuels these activities and aids recovery. However, with the plethora of dietary advice, fad diets, and nutrition information available, determining what to eat can be overwhelming. Enter AI: a tool that's transforming the way we approach nutrition, offering personalized meal plans tailored to individual needs, goals, and even genetic makeup.

One of the primary ways AI is revolutionizing nutrition is by calculating an individual's daily caloric needs based on factors like age, weight, height, activity level, and fitness goals. But it doesn't stop there. AI goes a step further by determining the optimal macronutrient distribution – the right balance of proteins, fats, and carbohydrates – ensuring that individuals not only consume the right amount of calories but also get them from the right sources.

Food Preferences and Dietary Restrictions: AI-driven nutrition platforms often come equipped with extensive food databases. Users can input their food preferences, allergies, and dietary restrictions. The AI then crafts meal plans that adhere to these specifications, ensuring that individuals enjoy their meals while still aligning with their nutritional goals.

Dynamic Meal Planning: Just as AI adjusts workout regimens based on feedback, it does the same for meal plans. If a user finds a particular meal unsatisfying or feels low on energy, they can provide this feedback. The AI then recalibrates, adjusting future meal plans to better suit the user's needs.

Integration with Fitness Goals: AI understands the intricate relationship between diet and fitness. For someone aiming for muscle gain, the AI might suggest a protein-rich diet. Conversely, for someone training for a marathon, it might emphasize carbohydrates to ensure sustained energy. This seamless integration ensures that the diet complements the fitness regimen, optimizing results.

Predictive Analysis for Optimal Health: Some advanced AI nutrition platforms can even predict potential future health issues based on current dietary habits. By analyzing patterns and comparing them with vast health and nutrition databases, AI can offer insights and suggest dietary changes to mitigate potential health risks.

Educational Insights: Beyond just suggesting meals, AI-driven platforms often provide educational insights. They explain the reasoning behind certain food choices, offer information on the nutritional content of meals, and even provide cooking tips and recipes. This empowers users, giving them the knowledge to make informed dietary decisions even outside the AI's recommendations.

The potential of AI in nutrition is vast. It offers a level of personalization previously unattainable, ensuring that individuals get the most out of their diets. But as we focus on fueling our bodies, it's equally crucial to address recovery and injury prevention. AI's role doesn't end at the dining table; it extends to rehabilitation, ensuring that individuals remain injury-free and at the peak of their fitness.

Rehabilitation and Recovery: AI's Role in Predicting and Preventing Injuries

In the realm of sports and fitness, injuries are an unfortunate reality. Whether it's a professional athlete or a casual gym-goer, the risk of injury looms large. However, with the advent of AI, the approach to injury prevention and rehabilitation is undergoing a transformative shift. By harnessing the power of data and predictive analytics, AI is playing a pivotal role in minimizing injury risks and optimizing recovery processes. Let's delve deeper into the specific ways AI is reshaping the landscape of injury prevention and rehabilitation, offering innovative solutions to age-old challenges.

Predictive Injury Analysis: One of the most groundbreaking applications of AI in sports medicine is its ability to predict potential injuries. By analyzing an individual's movement patterns, muscle imbalances, and biomechanics, AI can identify vulnerabilities that might lead to injuries. For instance, a runner with a slight imbalance in their gait might be at risk for a knee injury. AI can detect such nuances, allowing for preemptive interventions.

Personalized Rehabilitation Programs: Every injury is unique, and so is every individual's recovery journey. AI tailors rehabilitation exercises to the specific needs of the injured party. By analyzing data like range of motion, pain thresholds, and healing progress, AI can adjust and optimize the rehab regimen in real-time, ensuring a faster and more effective recovery.

Wearable Tech Integration: Wearable devices equipped with sensors can continuously monitor an individual's vitals, movements, and strain on specific muscles or joints. This data, when processed by AI, provides insights into when an athlete or individual might be overexerting themselves or if they're moving in a way that could lead to injury.

Virtual Physical Therapy: With advancements in AI and augmented reality, virtual physical therapy sessions are becoming a reality. Individuals can engage in guided rehab exercises from the comfort of their homes, with AI-powered systems providing real-time feedback on their form and progress.

Emphasis on Holistic Recovery: Beyond just physical recovery, AI recognizes the importance of mental well-being in the rehabilitation process. Some AI-driven platforms offer mindfulness exercises, sleep optimization tips, and stress-reducing techniques, understanding that a holistic approach accelerates recovery.

Continuous Learning and Adaptation: The beauty of AI lies in its ability to learn continuously. As more data gets fed into the system – be it from one individual or thousands – the AI becomes more adept at understanding injury patterns, refining its predictive capabilities, and enhancing its rehab recommendations.

The integration of AI in injury prevention and rehabilitation signifies a paradigm shift in sports medicine. It offers a proactive approach, ensuring that individuals can enjoy their fitness journeys while minimizing downtime due to injuries. However, the influence of AI in the sports domain isn't limited to the athletes or fitness enthusiasts alone. It extends to the spectators, revolutionizing the way fans engage with and experience sports.

AI in Enhancing Fan Engagement and Experience

In the realm of sports, the athletes and the games they play are undeniably the main attractions. However, the experience of the fans, both in-stadium and remotely, is equally paramount. As technology has evolved, so too has the fan experience, with Artificial Intelligence playing a central role in this transformation. From the way fans consume content to the immersive experiences they can now enjoy, AI is reshaping the landscape of sports viewership.

Virtual and Augmented Reality Experiences Powered by AI

The dawn of Virtual Reality (VR) and Augmented Reality (AR) has ushered in a new era of fan engagement. No longer limited to watching a game on television, fans can now immerse themselves in a 360-degree virtual environment, feeling as if they are right in the stadium or even on the field. AI enhances these

VR and AR experiences by analyzing real-time data, adjusting the virtual environment accordingly, and even predicting plays or outcomes based on historical data. This not only offers a more engaging viewing experience but also provides fans with insights and perspectives they wouldn't have access to otherwise.

Predictive Algorithms for Enhancing Live Game Broadcasts

Live game broadcasts have always been about more than just showing the game. They're about telling a story, providing context, and enhancing the viewing experience with stats, replays, and expert analysis. AI takes this to the next level. With predictive algorithms, broadcasts can now anticipate game outcomes, suggest potential strategies, and provide real-time analytics that were previously impossible to calculate on the fly. For instance, AI can analyze a basketball player's shooting form in real-time, predicting the likelihood of a shot being successful. Such insights not only enrich the viewing experience but also provide fans with a deeper understanding of the game's intricacies.

Personalized Content Delivery for Fans Based on Preferences

In today's digital age, content is king. However, with the sheer volume of content available, personalization becomes crucial. AI-driven platforms can analyze a fan's viewing history, social media interactions, and even in-app behaviors to curate a personalized content feed. Whether it's highlight reels of their favorite players, in-depth analyses of their preferred teams, or even behind-the-scenes content, AI ensures fans get what they're most interested in. This not only enhances fan loyalty but also ensures a more engaged and active viewership.

As we marvel at these advancements in fan engagement and experience, it's essential to recognize the broader implications of AI in sports. One such area where AI's influence is profoundly felt is in the training regimens of elite athletes, as we'll explore in the following case study.

Case Study: AI in Olympic Training Regimens

An In-depth Look at How Elite Athletes are Leveraging AI

The world of elite sports has always been a crucible of innovation. From advanced training techniques to cutting-edge equipment, athletes and their support teams have perpetually sought every possible advantage to enhance performance. In recent years, one of the most transformative tools to emerge in this quest for excellence is Artificial Intelligence.

Historically, the training of elite athletes was as much an art as it was a science. Coaches relied on their experience, intuition, and observational skills to guide their athletes to peak performance. While these elements remain crucial, the integration of AI has added a new dimension to training, offering insights that were previously unimaginable.

One of the primary ways AI has been integrated into elite training is through data collection and analysis. Every movement, every heartbeat, every stride an athlete takes can now be tracked, quantified, and analyzed. Wearable devices, such as smartwatches and fitness trackers, collect a plethora of data points, from heart rate to oxygen levels. High-speed cameras can capture an athlete's movement in minute detail, allowing for biomechanical analysis. Even an athlete's sleep and nutrition can be monitored and optimized using AI tools.

But collecting data is only the first step. The true power of AI lies in its ability to process this vast amount of information and extract meaningful insights from it. Machine learning algorithms can identify patterns and trends in an athlete's performance, pinpointing areas of strength and weakness. For instance, an AI system might analyze a swimmer's stroke and identify minute inefficiencies that, when corrected, could shave off crucial milliseconds from their time.

Beyond performance optimization, AI also plays a pivotal role in injury prevention. By analyzing an athlete's biomechanics and physiological data, AI systems can predict areas of potential strain or injury risk. This allows coaches and medical teams to intervene proactively, adjusting training regimens or recommending specific therapies to prevent injuries before they occur.

Furthermore, AI-driven simulations can also provide athletes with virtual training environments, allowing them to practice and hone their skills in a variety of scenarios. For example, a downhill skier can navigate a virtual representation of an Olympic course, with AI algorithms adjusting variables like snow conditions and visibility, preparing the athlete for any eventuality.

In essence, AI acts as a force multiplier in the training of elite athletes. It amplifies the capabilities of coaches, providing them with a depth and breadth of information that was previously out of reach. But as with any powerful tool, its use comes with responsibilities and considerations, especially when the stakes are as high as Olympic gold. As we delve deeper into this topic, we'll explore how AI integrates with biometrics and performance data to offer a holistic view of an athlete's capabilities.

The Integration of Biometrics, Performance Data, and AI Analytics

The fusion of biometrics, performance data, and AI analytics represents a paradigm shift in the world of elite sports training. This convergence is not just about collecting more data but about deriving actionable insights from it, insights that can redefine the boundaries of human performance.

Biometrics, at its core, is the measurement of physical and behavioral characteristics. In sports, this translates to metrics like heart rate, oxygen saturation, muscle activity, and even stress levels. These metrics provide a window into the athlete's physiological state, revealing how their body responds to different training intensities, conditions, and recovery periods.

Performance data, on the other hand, focuses on the output of the athlete. It encompasses metrics like speed, acceleration, power, and endurance. This data is often captured using a combination of wearable sensors, video analysis, and other specialized equipment. For instance, force plates can measure the power output of a sprinter's start, while motion capture technology can analyze the fluidity of a gymnast's routine.

The magic happens when these two data sets are combined and processed using AI analytics. AI algorithms can correlate biometric data with performance metrics, identifying the physiological conditions under which an athlete performs best. For example, an AI system might determine that a cyclist produces their maximum power output when their heart rate is between 160-170 beats per minute and their oxygen saturation is above 95%. Such insights allow for highly tailored training regimens, ensuring that athletes train in their optimal zones to maximize gains.

Moreover, AI analytics can also identify subtle patterns that might be missed by human observation. It might notice, for instance, that a tennis player's serve speed decreases slightly when their hydration levels drop below a certain point, or that a long-distance runner's stride becomes less efficient when their core temperature rises above a specific threshold. These nuanced insights can inform everything from nutrition and hydration strategies to the design of performance-enhancing sportswear.

Another transformative aspect of this integration is the ability for real-time feedback. Modern AI systems can process biometric and performance data in real-time, providing athletes and coaches with instant feedback during training sessions. This allows for on-the-spot adjustments, ensuring that every training session is as productive as possible.

In essence, the integration of biometrics, performance data, and AI analytics is creating a feedback loop of unprecedented precision in sports training. Every bead of sweat, every breath, every movement is captured, analyzed, and fed back into the training process, creating a cycle of continuous improvement.

As we transition to the next segment, we'll delve into the tangible outcomes of this integration. How have these AI-driven insights translated to the field, track, or court? And more importantly, how have they redefined what athletes are capable of achieving?

The Results: How AI-Driven Insights Have Led to Breakthrough Performances

The integration of AI in sports training isn't just a theoretical endeavor; it has already produced tangible results, pushing athletes to new heights and redefining what's possible in the realm of human performance.

One of the most significant outcomes of AI-driven insights is the enhancement of individualized training. Every athlete is unique, with distinct strengths, weaknesses, and physiological responses. AI's ability to analyze vast amounts of data has enabled coaches and trainers to tailor training regimens to the specific needs of each athlete. This hyper-personalized approach ensures that athletes are always training at their optimal level, leading to faster improvements and reduced risk of injuries.

For instance, in endurance sports like marathon running, AI has been instrumental in optimizing pacing strategies. By analyzing an athlete's biometric data and past performances, AI systems can predict the optimal pace for different segments of a race, ensuring that the athlete doesn't burn out too early or leave too much in reserve. This has led to numerous personal bests and even world record attempts.

In team sports, AI-driven insights have revolutionized game strategy. Basketball teams, for example, use AI to analyze the shooting patterns of opposing players, identifying their preferred spots on the court and their shooting percentages from different positions. This information is then used to devise defensive strategies, forcing players into less favorable shooting positions and increasing the team's chances of victory.

Another area where AI has made a significant impact is in injury prevention. By continuously monitoring an athlete's biometric data, AI systems can detect signs of fatigue or strain that might be precursors to more serious injuries. This allows coaches to adjust training loads or give athletes the necessary rest, ensuring that they remain in peak condition throughout the season.

The world of sports has always been about pushing the boundaries of human potential. With the aid of AI, these boundaries are being expanded like never before. Athletes are running faster, jumping higher, and performing at levels that were once thought to be unattainable. And as AI technology continues to evolve, it's exciting to think about the new frontiers that will be unlocked in the world of sports.

However, with these advancements come new challenges and considerations. As we delve into the next section, we'll explore the ethical implications of using AI in sports. How do we ensure fairness in competition when athletes have access to such advanced tools? What about the privacy concerns related to collecting and analyzing vast amounts of biometric data? And, most importantly, how do we preserve the spirit of competition in an age of technological augmentation?

Ethical Considerations: Fairness, Data Privacy, and the Spirit of Competition

The integration of AI in sports, while promising, brings forth a myriad of ethical dilemmas. As with any technological advancement, it's crucial to strike a balance between harnessing its potential and preserving the core values that define sports. To delve deeper into this, let's explore some of the primary ethical challenges and considerations that arise with the integration of AI in sports:"

Fairness in Competition:

The primary concern is ensuring a level playing field. If certain teams or athletes have access to more advanced

AI tools than others, it could lead to an uneven advantage. This disparity can be particularly pronounced between wealthy teams or countries and those with fewer resources. The question then arises: Should there be standardized regulations on the type of AI tools that can be used in training and competition? And if so, who should be responsible for setting and enforcing these standards?

Data Privacy:

With AI-driven training relying heavily on the collection of biometric data, there are valid concerns about data privacy and security. Athletes' health and performance data are sensitive, and there's a risk of misuse if it falls into the wrong hands. Moreover, who owns this data? Is it the athlete, the team, or the organization that provided the AI tool? Clear guidelines and robust data protection measures are essential to address these concerns.

The Spirit of Competition:

Sports, at its core, is a celebration of human potential and spirit. With the increasing reliance on AI and technology, there's a risk of overshadowing the human element. How much of an athlete's success can be attributed to their natural talent and hard work versus the AI tools they used? And does relying on AI diminish the value of their achievements? It's a delicate balance to maintain, ensuring that technology aids human performance rather than defining it.

Informed Consent:

Before collecting data or implementing AI-driven training regimens, athletes should be fully informed about the processes, potential risks, and benefits. They should have the autonomy to decide whether or not to use these tools, without any external pressures.

Accessibility and Inclusivity:

As AI becomes more integrated into sports, it's crucial to ensure that it doesn't become a tool exclusive to the elite. Efforts should be made to democratize access to AI tools, ensuring that athletes at all levels, from grassroots to professional, can benefit from the advancements.

In conclusion, while AI offers unprecedented opportunities to revolutionize the world of sports and fitness, it's essential to approach its integration with caution, keeping ethical considerations at the forefront. The goal should always be to enhance human potential, not overshadow it. As we move forward into this new era, stakeholders in the sports industry, from governing bodies to athletes, will need to collaborate, ensuring that the spirit of sportsmanship remains undiminished in the age of AI.

Chapter 12: AI in Mental Health and Well-being

In recent years, the global conversation around mental health has shifted dramatically. Once a topic shrouded in stigma and misunderstanding, mental well-being has emerged as a paramount concern in the 21st century. The World Health Organization now recognizes depression as the leading cause of disability worldwide. As societies grapple with the complexities of mental health challenges, the urgency for innovative solutions has never been greater.

Enter technology. The digital age has ushered in a plethora of tools and platforms aimed at addressing mental health. From meditation apps to online therapy platforms, technology has bridged gaps, offering support to those who might have previously suffered in silence. But as with many sectors, the most transformative shifts are being driven by the advent of Artificial Intelligence. AI's ability to analyze vast amounts of data, recognize patterns, and adapt in real-time positions it as a game-changer in the realm of mental health support.

However, the marriage of AI and mental health isn't without its skeptics. Questions arise: Can a machine truly understand the human psyche? Can algorithms replace the nuanced understanding and empathy of a human therapist? While these concerns are valid, there's no denying the potential AI holds in revolutionizing mental health care, especially in areas where human resources are limited or inaccessible.

As we delve deeper into this chapter, we'll explore the multifaceted ways AI is making waves in the mental health sector, from virtual therapists to predictive tools that can preemptively identify potential mental health crises. The intersection of AI and mental health is a testament to technology's potential to not just improve lives but to profoundly transform them.

With the stage set, let's begin by examining some of the most groundbreaking AI-driven therapeutic tools that are redefining the boundaries of mental health support.

AI-driven Therapeutic Tools: Chatbots, Virtual Therapists, and Mood Prediction

The realm of mental health, traditionally reliant on human interaction and intuition, might seem an unlikely candidate for AI intervention. Yet, the sheer scale of mental health challenges globally demands innovative solutions that can scale and adapt. AI-driven tools, with their ability to process vast amounts of data and offer real-time responses, are stepping up to this challenge. Building on this technological momentum, several key developments have emerged in the realm of AI-driven mental health solutions. These include:

1. Chatbots: The 24/7 Mental Health Assistant

One of the most immediate applications of AI in mental health has been the development of therapeutic chatbots. These are designed to provide instant, round-the-clock support to individuals in need. Platforms like Replika, Wysa, and others use natural language processing (NLP) to engage users in conversations, offering immediate feedback, coping strategies, or simply a virtual ear to vent to. While they don't replace human therapists, they fill a crucial gap, especially during off-hours or for those hesitant to seek traditional therapy.

2. Virtual Therapists: Bridging the Human-AI Gap

Beyond chatbots, more sophisticated AI-driven platforms are emerging that mimic the experience of a human therapist. Using advanced algorithms, these virtual therapists can recognize emotional cues, offer therapeutic interventions, and even guide users through cognitive-behavioral exercises. Ellie, developed by the Institute for Creative Technologies, is one such example. While interacting with users, Ellie analyzes verbal and non-verbal cues to provide tailored feedback, making the experience deeply personalized.

3. Mood Prediction: A Proactive Approach

One of the most promising avenues of AI in mental health is its potential for mood prediction. By analyzing data points from a user's digital footprint—like social media activity, text messages, or even voice tone in phone calls—AI tools can predict potential mood shifts. Apps like Moodpath or eQuoo use such data to offer users insights into their emotional well-being, potentially identifying depressive or anxious episodes before they escalate.

The advantages of these AI-driven tools are manifold. They offer immediacy, scalability, and, in many cases, affordability. For individuals living in areas with limited mental health resources or those who face barriers like stigma, these tools can be life-changing. However, they also raise questions. How do we ensure the quality of AI-driven interventions? How do we navigate the fine line between tech support and human empathy?

As we transition from these tools, it's essential to recognize that while AI offers incredible potential in mental health support, its true power lies in personalization. The next section delves into how AI is tailoring interventions to individual needs, ensuring that mental health support is as unique as the individuals seeking it.

Personalized Mental Health: Tailoring Interventions Using AI

The beauty of mental health care lies in its deeply personal nature. Every individual's mental health journey is unique, shaped by a myriad of factors including genetics, environment, experiences, and personal beliefs. Traditional therapeutic approaches have always emphasized the importance of individualized care, understanding that what works for one person might not work for another. With the advent of AI in mental health, the potential for personalization has reached unprecedented levels. Delving deeper into this realm, we can identify several pivotal areas where AI's influence is making a marked difference. These encompass:

1. Data-Driven Insights for Tailored Care

The foundation of AI's personalization capability is its ability to process vast amounts of data quickly. By analyzing an individual's digital interactions, physiological metrics (like heart rate or sleep patterns), and even responses during therapeutic sessions, AI can generate insights into an individual's mental state. These insights can then inform tailored interventions. For instance, if an AI tool detects patterns of insomnia and increased social media activity late at night, it might suggest interventions related to sleep hygiene or digital detox.

2. Dynamic Therapy Modules

AI-driven platforms can adapt therapeutic modules based on real-time feedback. For example, if a user is engaging with a cognitive-behavioral therapy (CBT) module on an app and finds certain exercises particularly challenging or triggering, the AI can adjust the subsequent sessions to be more supportive or approach the topic differently. This dynamic adjustment ensures that the therapeutic journey aligns closely with the user's pace and comfort.

3. Predictive Interventions

One of the most groundbreaking potentials of AI in personalized mental health is its predictive capability. By recognizing patterns that might indicate a potential decline in mental well-being, AI tools can proactively suggest interventions. This could range from recommending relaxation exercises when stress levels spike to suggesting a check-in with a therapist if patterns indicate a potential depressive episode.

4. Integration with Other Health Metrics

Mental health doesn't exist in a vacuum. It's closely intertwined with physical health, and AI's ability to integrate data from various health metrics can offer a holistic view of an individual's well-being. For instance, by analyzing data from fitness trackers, dietary logs, and mental health apps, AI can provide insights into how physical activity or diet impacts mental well-being and vice versa.

While the potential of AI in offering personalized mental health interventions is vast, it's essential to approach it with a balanced perspective. AI tools are, at their core, algorithms. They lack the human touch, the intuitive understanding, and the empathetic connection that forms the bedrock of mental health care. However, when used as a supplementary tool, AI can enhance the therapeutic process, making it more responsive and attuned to individual needs.

As we delve deeper into the world of AI-driven mental health tools, it's worth exploring specific examples that have made a mark. One such tool that has garnered attention for its innovative approach and tangible impact is Woebot. Let's dive into this case study to understand how AI is making waves in the therapeutic landscape.

Case Study: Woebot – The AI Therapist and its Impact

In the vast landscape of AI-driven mental health tools, Woebot stands out not just for its innovative approach but also for the tangible impact it has had on its users. Developed by a team of Stanford psychologists, Woebot is a chatbot designed to offer cognitive-behavioral therapy (CBT) interventions to users in real-time. But what makes Woebot so special, and how has it influenced the broader conversation about AI in mental health?

The Genesis of Woebot

Woebot was born out of a simple realization: while the demand for mental health services is soaring, access remains a significant barrier for many. Traditional therapy can be expensive, and in many regions, mental health professionals are in short supply. Woebot was envisioned as a bridge – a tool that could offer immediate, affordable, and effective CBT interventions to anyone with a smartphone.

How Woebot Works

At its core, Woebot is a chatbot. Users can engage in text-based conversations with the bot, discussing their feelings, challenges, and concerns. Drawing from a vast database of CBT techniques, Woebot responds with insights, exercises, and strategies tailored to the user's current state. Over time, the bot learns from these interactions, refining its responses to better suit the individual's needs.

The Impact

Several studies have explored Woebot's efficacy. One notable study found that users who interacted with Woebot regularly experienced a significant reduction in depressive symptoms compared to a control group. Beyond the numbers, user testimonials highlight the bot's role in offering immediate support, especially during moments of acute distress.

Challenges and Criticisms

While Woebot has been lauded for its innovative approach, it hasn't been without criticism. Some mental health professionals express concerns about over-reliance on such tools, emphasizing that a chatbot can never replace the nuanced understanding and empathetic connection a human therapist offers. Additionally, there are concerns about data privacy and the potential misuse of sensitive information shared with the bot.

The Future of Woebot

The team behind Woebot envisions a future where the bot becomes even more refined in its interactions, offering more personalized and effective interventions. They also see potential in integrating Woebot with other digital health tools, creating a holistic ecosystem for mental well-being.

Woebot's journey from a Stanford project to a globally recognized mental health tool underscores the transformative potential of AI in mental health. However, as with all innovations, it brings forth a slew of ethical considerations. As we venture further into the realm of AI-driven mental health interventions, it's imperative to tread with caution, ensuring that the very tools designed to support well-being don't inadvertently harm it.

Ethical Considerations: Privacy, Effectiveness, and the Human Touch in Therapy

The integration of AI into mental health care is undeniably transformative, promising increased accessibility, affordability, and personalization. However, as with all technological advancements, it brings forth a set of ethical dilemmas that must be addressed to ensure the well-being of users. This section delves into the primary ethical concerns surrounding AI-driven mental health interventions.

1. Privacy and Data Security

Data Sensitivity: Mental health data is deeply personal. Sharing one's innermost thoughts, feelings, and struggles requires a significant level of trust. When AI tools are involved, there's a risk that this sensitive data could be mishandled or misused.

Potential for Breaches: No system is entirely immune to cyber threats. A breach in an AI mental health tool could expose users' intimate details, leading to potential harm, stigma, or discrimination.

Data Usage: There's also the question of how this data is used. Is it solely for therapeutic purposes, or could it be monetized, shared, or used for other non-disclosed reasons?

2. Effectiveness and Reliability

Over-reliance: There's a danger that individuals might over-rely on AI tools, sidelining traditional therapy methods that might be more effective for them.

Accuracy: AI is only as good as the data it's trained on. If the algorithms underpinning these tools are based on limited or biased data, their recommendations or interventions might not be universally applicable or effective.

Accountability: In cases where AI-driven advice or intervention leads to adverse outcomes, who is held accountable? The developers? The therapists who recommended the tool? Or is it chalked up to machine error?

3. The Human Touch in Therapy

Empathy and Understanding: While AI can mimic human conversation patterns, it lacks genuine empathy and understanding. For many, the therapeutic process's success hinges on the human connection, the feeling of being truly understood and supported.

Complexity of Human Emotion: Emotions and mental health challenges are multifaceted. Can an AI truly grasp the depth and breadth of human emotion, especially when nuances, contradictions, and complexities come into play?

Depersonalization: There's a risk that the therapeutic process becomes depersonalized. Instead of tailored interventions based on deep human understanding, users might receive generic, algorithm-driven responses.

4. Equity and Access

While AI tools promise increased accessibility, there's a risk they might further widen the mental health care gap. Those with the means might access advanced, premium AI tools, while others might be left with basic or even subpar solutions.

5. The Therapist's Role

As AI becomes more integrated into mental health care, the role of human therapists might evolve. There's a potential for job displacement or a shift in job roles, leading to ethical and professional dilemmas.

In summary, the marriage of AI and mental health care is filled with potential, but it's a delicate balance. Ensuring that these tools are developed and used ethically is paramount. As we stand on this frontier, it's crucial to prioritize human well-being above all, ensuring that technology serves as a tool, not a replacement, for genuine human connection and understanding.

Conclusion

As we've traversed the landscape of AI's role in mental health and well-being, it's evident that we're on the cusp of a revolution. The potential benefits are vast: increased accessibility, personalized interventions, and innovative therapeutic tools that can reach individuals in ways traditional therapy might not. The promise of a world where mental health support is available at the click of a button, tailored to individual needs, and constantly evolving based on real-time feedback is tantalizing.

However, with great potential comes great responsibility. The ethical considerations we've discussed underscore the importance of proceeding with caution. The very essence of mental health care is rooted in trust, empathy, and understanding. As we integrate AI into this realm, we must ensure that these foundational principles are not overshadowed by the allure of technology.

Furthermore, while AI offers novel solutions, it also surfaces age-old challenges in new forms: the need for privacy, the quest for genuine human connection, and the ethical dilemmas of introducing new technologies into sensitive areas of human life.

As we move forward, a collaborative approach is essential. Technologists, therapists, patients, and policymakers must come together to shape the future of AI in mental health. By doing so, we can harness the power of AI to enhance mental health care while preserving the human touch that lies at its heart.

In the end, the goal remains unchanged: to support and uplift the mental well-being of individuals. Whether through traditional means or AI-driven tools, the focus should always be on the individual's holistic well-being, ensuring that every person has access to the care and support they need.

Chapter 13: The Dystopian Future: When AI Goes Too Far

In the annals of human history, few innovations have captured our collective imagination as intensely as Artificial Intelligence. From the earliest days of computing, the idea of creating machines that could think, learn, and perhaps even feel like humans has been a tantalizing prospect. The allure of AI lies in its promise: a world where mundane tasks are automated, where complex problems are solved in the blink of an eye, and where humanity can leverage this power to ascend to new heights of progress and understanding.

Yet, as with all powerful tools, there's a flip side. The same technology that can be used to diagnose diseases, predict natural disasters, and enhance our daily lives can also be harnessed for more nefarious purposes. The fear is not just about machines taking over jobs, but about them taking over everything. What happens when the tools we've built to serve us no longer just work alongside us but start making decisions for us? What if these decisions aren't in our best interest?

Science fiction has long played with these themes, painting pictures of dystopian futures where machines rule with an iron fist, and humanity is subjugated or even eradicated. While these narratives might seem far-fetched, they touch on genuine concerns that many experts in the field share. As AI systems grow more sophisticated, the balance of power could shift in ways we haven't fully anticipated.

The journey into the world of AI is akin to opening Pandora's box. The potential benefits are vast, but so are the risks. As we stand on the precipice of this new era, it's crucial to tread with caution, ensuring that the balance of power remains in human hands.

As we delve deeper into this chapter, we'll explore the potential trajectories AI might take if left unchecked. First, let's examine the possible rise of machines and how unchecked AI development could tilt the scales of power.

The rapid evolution of AI is akin to a double-edged sword. On one side, it offers unparalleled advancements in various sectors, from healthcare to finance, promising a brighter future. On the other, it poses significant risks, especially if its development remains unchecked. The potential for AI to shift the balance of power, both in terms of geopolitics and within societies, is a concern that cannot be overlooked.

Centralization of Power: One of the most immediate risks of unchecked AI development is the centralization of power. As AI systems become more integral to various sectors, those who control these systems wield significant influence. This could lead to a scenario where a few tech giants or nations with advanced AI capabilities dominate the global landscape, pushing out competitors and establishing a form of techno-oligarchy.

Economic Disparities: The integration of AI into industries can lead to massive job displacements. While new roles will emerge, the transition might not be smooth, leading to economic disparities. Those with AI skills and resources could thrive, while others could face unemployment, widening the gap between the 'haves' and the 'have-nots'.

Autonomous Weapons: One of the more alarming prospects is the development of AI-powered autonomous weapons. These machines, capable of making life-or-death decisions without human intervention, could change the face of warfare. In the wrong hands, they could be used to suppress populations or wage wars with unprecedented precision and scale.

Decision-making Dominance: As organizations and governments increasingly rely on AI for decision-making, there's a risk that these systems, with their inherent biases, could make choices that don't necessarily benefit the broader population. From criminal sentencing to loan approvals, if AI's decision-making processes aren't transparent and accountable, they could perpetuate inequalities and injustices.

Loss of Privacy: With AI's capability to process vast amounts of data, there's a potential for invasive surveillance. This isn't just about governments spying on citizens but also about corporations using AI to mine personal data for profit, often without explicit consent.

Ethical Dilemmas: As AI systems make more decisions, ethical dilemmas will arise. For instance, in the case of autonomous vehicles, how should the AI decide in a no-win scenario? Whose life should be prioritized? These questions don't have easy answers, and if not addressed, could lead to societal unrest.

While these scenarios paint a grim picture, it's essential to remember that they represent potential outcomes, not certainties. The future of AI is not set in stone, and with the right checks and balances, these risks can be mitigated. However, the first step in preventing such outcomes is recognizing and understanding them.

As we move forward, it's crucial to delve deeper into one of the most pressing concerns related to unchecked AI development: the creation of an omnipresent surveillance society. Let's explore this further.

In the annals of science fiction, the concept of a surveillance state often takes center stage, painting a picture of a world where every move is watched, every word is heard, and privacy is but a distant memory. While this might have seemed far-fetched a few decades ago, the rapid advancements in AI and data analytics are bringing us closer to such a reality.

The All-Seeing Eye: With the proliferation of cameras in public spaces, combined with AI-driven facial recognition technology, it's becoming increasingly feasible to track individuals in real-time. Cities like Beijing are already deploying vast networks of surveillance cameras that can identify and track individuals based on their facial features.

Digital Footprints: Our online activities, from the websites we visit to the messages we send, leave behind digital footprints. AI algorithms can analyze these footprints to create detailed profiles, predicting everything from our shopping habits to our political inclinations.

Voice Recognition and Eavesdropping: Smart devices equipped with voice assistants, like Amazon's Alexa or Google Home, are becoming household staples. While they offer convenience, they also have the potential to eavesdrop, with AI algorithms processing our conversations to serve us better – or to serve better-targeted advertisements.

Predictive Policing: Law enforcement agencies are exploring the use of AI to predict criminal activities. By analyzing vast datasets, from social media posts to public records, AI can potentially forecast where a crime might occur or who might commit it. While this could lead to a reduction in crime rates, it also poses significant ethical concerns, especially if misused.

Social Credit Systems: Drawing inspiration from financial credit scores, some nations are exploring the idea of a social credit system. Here, AI analyzes an individual's behavior, both online and offline, to assign a 'score.' This score could then influence everything from loan approvals to job opportunities.

The Loss of Anonymity: With AI-driven surveillance, the very notion of anonymity is under threat. Whether you're attending a public rally or just taking a walk in the park, the chances of you being 'anonymous' in such a world are slim.

While the potential benefits of such a surveillance system, like reduced crime rates and enhanced public safety, are undeniable, they come at a significant cost. The erosion of personal privacy, the potential misuse of data by authoritarian regimes, and the psychological impact of constantly being 'watched' are just a few of the challenges posed by an AI-driven surveillance state.

The implications of such a surveillance-centric society are vast and varied. To better understand the potential outcomes, let's delve into a hypothetical scenario of an AI-driven city and its broader implications.

Case Study: A Hypothetical Scenario of an AI-Driven City and Its Implications

Neo-Utopia: The City of Tomorrow

In the not-so-distant future, imagine a city named Neo-Utopia, hailed as the pinnacle of technological advancement. Every aspect of this city, from its infrastructure to its governance, is driven by sophisticated AI systems. At first glance, Neo-Utopia appears to be a dream come true, a perfect blend of efficiency, safety, and convenience. But as we delve deeper, the complexities and challenges of such a city begin to surface.

Seamless Transportation: The city's transportation system is entirely autonomous. AI-driven cars, buses, and trains ensure punctuality, safety, and optimal routing. Traffic jams are a thing of the past, and accidents are rare, thanks to the interconnected network of vehicles communicating with each other in real-time.

Energy Efficiency: AI algorithms optimize energy consumption. Buildings adjust their temperature settings based on occupancy and weather predictions. Streetlights dim when no one is around and brighten as someone approaches.

Crime Prevention: The city's law enforcement uses predictive policing. AI systems analyze data to predict where a crime is likely to occur, dispatching drones or robotic patrols to those areas. Cameras with facial recognition are omnipresent, making it nearly impossible for any criminal to go unnoticed.

Healthcare Revolution: AI-driven health pods are scattered throughout the city. Residents can step in for a quick health check-up, with AI systems analyzing vitals, predicting potential health issues, and even dispensing medication.

Governance and Decision Making: The city council uses AI to analyze public opinion, gather feedback, and even make certain administrative decisions. Voting on local issues is done digitally, with AI ensuring the integrity of the process.

Personalized Services: From shopping to entertainment, AI tailors every experience. Digital billboards change advertisements based on who's looking at them. Restaurants make meal suggestions based on a person's health data and past preferences.

However, beneath this veneer of perfection lie some unsettling truths.

Privacy Concerns: In Neo-Utopia, anonymity is non-existent. Every movement, purchase, and even conversation can be tracked and analyzed. The city's residents have traded their privacy for convenience.

Economic Disparities: While AI has brought about numerous conveniences, it has also led to job losses in sectors like transportation and retail. The divide between the tech-savvy elite and the rest grows wider.

Mental Health Issues: The constant surveillance and lack of privacy can lead to anxiety and stress. The feeling of always being watched and the pressure to conform to societal norms, as dictated by AI analytics, can be overwhelming.

Loss of Human Touch: While the city's systems are efficient, they lack the human touch. Interpersonal relationships suffer, and the city's residents often feel isolated, despite being constantly connected.

Neo-Utopia serves as a cautionary tale of what could happen if we let AI run unchecked. While the technological marvels of such a city are undeniable, they come at a cost. The challenge lies in finding a balance, ensuring that while we harness the power of AI, we don't lose the essence of what makes us human.

As we reflect on the implications of an AI-dominated society, it's essential to consider how humanity might respond. Would we passively accept this new reality, or would we seek ways to reclaim our autonomy and agency? Let's explore humanity's potential responses to such a future.

Humanity's Response: Resistance, Adaptation, and the Quest to Reclaim Control

The rise of AI, as illustrated by the hypothetical city of Neo-Utopia, presents both unprecedented opportunities and profound challenges. As with any significant technological shift, humanity's response is multifaceted, ranging from enthusiastic embrace to cautious skepticism and outright resistance.

Resistance Movements: In various parts of the world, resistance movements emerge, advocating for a return to a simpler, less AI-dominated life. These groups, often labeled as "Neo-Luddites," rally against the pervasive surveillance and loss of privacy. They establish "AI-free zones," communities where people live without the constant oversight of AI systems, emphasizing human connection, manual labor, and traditional ways of life.

Adaptive Integration: A more moderate response is seen in those who seek to integrate AI into their lives judiciously. They recognize the benefits of AI but are also acutely aware of its pitfalls. Efforts are made to ensure that AI systems are transparent, ethical, and accountable. Schools and institutions begin offering courses on "Digital Mindfulness," teaching individuals how to use AI tools without becoming overly reliant on them.

Regulatory Oversight: Governments worldwide grapple with the challenge of regulating AI. Comprehensive legislation is introduced to protect citizens' rights, especially concerning privacy and data ownership. International coalitions form, aiming to set global standards for AI development and deployment, ensuring that no single entity or AI becomes too powerful.

Technological Countermeasures: As AI systems become more sophisticated, so do the tools designed to counteract their more intrusive aspects. Innovators develop "AI shields" – software designed to protect individuals from unwanted surveillance, giving them more control over their digital footprint.

Emphasis on Human Values: A cultural renaissance emerges, emphasizing the qualities that make us uniquely human. Arts, humanities, and social sciences experience a resurgence in popularity, as society recognizes the importance of preserving human creativity, empathy, and intuition in an increasingly automated world.

Collaborative Coexistence: Many forward-thinkers advocate for a future where humans and AI coexist collaboratively. They envision a world where AI handles mundane tasks, while humans focus on creative, empathetic, and complex problem-solving endeavors. This perspective sees AI not as a replacement but as a tool that can amplify human potential.

In summary, the journey of AI, from its inception to its potential future, is a testament to human ingenuity and our relentless pursuit of progress. However, as we stand on the precipice of an AI-dominated future, we are reminded of the age-old adage: "With great power comes great responsibility."

The dystopian scenarios, while cautionary, are not inevitable. They serve as a reminder that the future is not something that happens to us; it's something we create. As we continue to integrate AI into our lives, our challenge is to do so in a way that upholds our values, preserves our rights, and enriches the human experience.

The story of AI is, in many ways, the story of humanity itself – a tale of ambition, innovation, challenges, and hope. As we move forward, our collective responsibility is to ensure that this story has a happy ending, not just for us, but for generations to come.

Conclusion: Navigating the AI Frontier

From its inception, Artificial Intelligence has been a subject of fascination, promise, and sometimes, trepidation. What began as theoretical constructs and rudimentary algorithms has now evolved into a force that is reshaping the very fabric of our society. The journey of AI, as chronicled in this book, has been nothing short of remarkable. From the foundational principles laid down by pioneers in the field to the groundbreaking innovations of today, AI has consistently pushed the boundaries of what's possible.

Across the chapters, we've seen the transformative impact of AI in myriad sectors. In our daily lives, AI-driven applications have become ubiquitous, simplifying tasks and offering unprecedented convenience. Economically, AI has catalyzed growth, driven innovation, and opened up new avenues for business. The realms of space exploration and the arts, seemingly poles apart, have both felt the touch of AI, leading to discoveries and creations that were once the stuff of science fiction.

As we stand on the cusp of an era where AI's influence is set to grow even further, it's essential to take a moment to reflect, not just on its achievements, but also on the challenges it presents.

The Double-Edged Sword

Artificial Intelligence, for all its promise, is a double-edged sword. On one hand, it holds the potential to revolutionize industries, make breakthroughs in scientific research, and elevate the quality of life for many. On the other, it brings forth challenges, ethical dilemmas, and questions about its unchecked growth. Can a machine ever truly replicate human creativity in art? What happens when AI-driven surveillance infringes on individual privacy? These are but a few of the myriad questions that arise.

It's crucial, then, to approach AI with a balanced perspective. While we harness its immense benefits, we must also remain vigilant of its pitfalls. Blindly racing ahead in the name of progress without considering the ethical and societal implications can lead to unforeseen consequences. As we've seen in various chapters, the key lies in collaboration – between humans and machines, policymakers and technologists, ethics and innovation.

Humanity at the Center

As we navigate the AI frontier, it's paramount to remember that technology, no matter how advanced, should serve humanity and not the other way around. The essence of AI's potential lies not just in its computational prowess but in its ability to augment, enhance, and respect human values, ethics, and well-being.

Throughout this book, we've encountered numerous instances where the human touch made all the difference. Whether it was the ethical considerations in mental health AI applications or the collaborative efforts between artists and AI in creating masterpieces, the human element remained irreplaceable. In the realm of sports and fitness, while AI provided invaluable insights, it was the human spirit, determination, and resilience that shone through. Similarly, in space exploration, while AI-driven rovers and satellites explored distant terrains, it was human curiosity and quest for knowledge that propelled these missions.

These examples underscore a fundamental truth: AI is a tool, and its true potential is realized when it's wielded with human insight, empathy, and purpose.

The Road Ahead: Responsibility and Collaboration

As we stand on the brink of an AI-augmented future, the responsibility of shaping this technology's trajectory doesn't lie with a select few. It's a shared responsibility, one that involves developers, policymakers, industries, and the general public. Every stakeholder has a role to play in ensuring that AI's evolution is aligned with the broader good of humanity.

International collaboration will be pivotal in this journey. In a world where technology knows no borders, setting global standards for AI development and deployment becomes crucial. Collaborative efforts can ensure that the benefits of AI are distributed equitably, preventing power imbalances and fostering a sense of global community.

As we move forward, the mantra should be clear: AI, driven by human values and steered by collaborative efforts, can lead to a future where technology truly serves humanity, enhancing our lives in ways we've yet to imagine.

Final Thoughts: The Future is Ours to Shape

As we close this exploration into the vast and intricate world of artificial intelligence, it's impossible not to be awed by the sheer potential this technology holds. From the microcosms of our daily lives to the expansive realms of space, AI promises to redefine the boundaries of what's possible, opening doors to opportunities we've only dared to dream of.

Yet, amidst this whirlwind of innovation and transformation, a fundamental truth remains: the essence of our future is not just in the algorithms or machines, but in our hands. AI, with all its prowess, is but a tool—a reflection of our aspirations, ambitions, and values. It's a canvas upon which we can paint, and the brushstrokes we choose will determine the picture that emerges.

This is a call to optimism, but also to vigilance. The horizon is filled with promise, but it's up to us to ensure that the dawn we're moving towards is one of hope, inclusivity, and prosperity. It's a future where technology doesn't overshadow humanity but uplifts it, where AI is not a master but a partner.

As you turn the final pages of this book, remember that the discourse on AI is ever-evolving, and your voice matters. Stay informed, remain engaged, and be proactive. Challenge, question, and dream. For in this dance between man and machine, it's the human spirit that leads. And with that spirit, we can ensure that the symphony of the future is harmonious, with technology serving as a force for unequivocal good.